SAMUEL SMILES'

SELF-HELP

SAMUEL SMILES'
SELF-HELP

A 52 BRILLIANT IDEAS INTERPRETATION
BY STEVE SHIPSIDE

First published in 2009 by
Infinite Ideas Limited
36 St Giles
Oxford
OX1 3LD
United Kingdom
www.infideas.com

A CIP catalogue record for this book is available from the British Library

ISBN 978-1-905940-96-7

Designed and typeset by Cylinder
Printed in India

BRILLIANT IDEAS

INTRODUCTION

It may seem ironic to start a book on self-help by pointing out the limitations of self-help books but there's no doubt that Samuel Smiles would have done just that. He was keenly aware of the difference between theorising about life and experiencing it first hand and was at pains to insist that *Self-help* was a collection of illustrations from life rather than a distillation, a short cut, a magic bullet: *'Useful and instructive though good reading may be, it is yet only one mode of cultivating the mind; and is much less influential than practical experience and good example in the formation of character.'*

As such he would probably have been horrified to walk into a modern bookshop and see an entire section of self-help books, large numbers of which seem to promise an entirely new life just by the reading of them. Smiles' interpretation of 'self-help' (a term he may be responsible for popularising) was with an emphasis on the 'self', i.e. that it was by your own efforts alone that you raised yourself from the common crowd. *Self-help* is a collection of examples of those who achieved greatness by perseverance, application, and bucketloads of back-breaking hard work. He even frowned on the idea of being helped by others, believing that a path made easier by others would not reap the same rewards.

If that sounds austere and Victorian it's because it is. Smiles was the very model of a Victorian man gathering up the stories and attributes of upstanding, industrious and virtuous men for the 'edification' (he wasn't too hot on 'entertainment') of his readers. Because he believed that nobility was to be found in all walks of life, his advice is as much for the leaders of men as for the followers of others. And, since he believed that the 'great' pay as much attention to the finest details as they do to the most important strategy, he offered advice on everything from personal finances to the winning of wars. So this book is about simultaneously helping yourself to be a better person, a better worker, and a better leader.

A bestseller since its appearance in 1859, *Self-help* went on to be one of the most popular non-fiction titles of the century. Smiles' conclusions that a gentleman was made not born, and that greatness was in everyone's reach – regardless of how humble their origins – must have made for compelling reading at a time when an industrial nation was reinventing itself, its role models and the balance of world power.

His time and culture, however, also meant he selected such models from people very much like himself (white, European and male), which seems out of sync with modern business books. With his evident dislike of 'amusement' ('*... there is a mania for frivolity and entertainment ...*'), I imagine he would have had apoplectic fits over business self-help guides like *Who moved my cheese?* or *Don't sweat the small stuff*.

Austere, unsmiling Victorianism is pretty hard stuff to digest these days but a great deal of the content of *Self-help* has not dated because it refers to the timeless – the essential – qualities of great people. Smiles would not have approved of the Infinite Ideas approach of making his book more accessible, but then in Smiles' day, information overload was when you accidentally bought two copies of the newspaper instead of one. He would, however, have approved of the emphasis on turning learning into practical application; so, perhaps the 'Here's an idea for you' features that accompany each brilliant idea would have helped bring Smiles back onside. He believed that theoretical knowledge without practical application was mere learning rather than wisdom and that the latter was worth far more than the former. So while Smiles would have preferred to make the process harder for you, he would at least have approved of the end goal.

1 LEARNING VERSUS WISDOM

'It is also to be borne in mind that the experience gathered from books, though often valuable, is but of the nature of learning; whereas the experience gained from actual life is of the nature of wisdom; and a small store of the latter is worth vastly more than any stock of the former,' asserts Samuel Smiles.

DEFINING IDEA...

Whatever study tends neither directly nor indirectly to make us better men and citizens, is at best but a specious and ingenious sort of idleness, and the knowledge we acquire by it only a creditable kind of ignorance – nothing more.
~ LORD BOLINGBROKE, STATESMAN

Though a great admirer of wisdom, Smiles argued strongly that mere learning is not only potentially worthless but also even harmful, and quotes 'Robertson of Brighton' as saying that *'multifarious reading weakens the mind like smoking'*. It's a deliciously disapproving phrase and a reminder that a lot of Victorian judgements seem to have been handed down by men who were permanently sucking lemons. Smiles, however, if not actually living up to his name, was at least not a lemon sucker by nature.

His point was that we can blind ourselves with science by learning without applying it: *'There is really no more personal merit attaching to the possession of superior intellectual powers than there is in the succession to a large estate. How are those powers used – how is that estate employed?'* No amount of management science, self-help books, or off-site seminars are going to bring success if they are not applied practically to the job in hand. Worse still, they can be distracting with businesspeople bouncing theories around in meetings like an elaborate word game.

Smiles has no time for knowledge for knowledge's sake, instead declaring that *'the object of knowledge should be to mature wisdom and improve character, to render us better, happier, and more useful; more benevolent, more energetic, and more efficient in the pursuit of every high purpose in life.'*

In short, if you're not reading this book with a view to being a more productive and successful human being then put it down at once and go and do something more useful instead. Smiles had no time for theorists and thinkers unless they were also doers who craved learning to apply it to their craft or art. There is a tendency to admire those with more learning than ourselves, in business as in general life. Smiles would have said that if those people aren't applying their knowledge, or becoming better and happier for it, then they do not deserve that admiration: *'Many indulge themselves in the conceit that they are cultivating their minds when they are only employed in the humbler occupation of killing time.'*

HERE'S AN IDEA FOR YOU...

There are 52 ideas in this book. Every time you find one that fits you, add it to your 'to do' list. Put the best idea of the day at the top of your list for tomorrow. If you haven't turned a single one of Smiles' ideas into reality after finishing the book you deserve to be haunted by sour-faced Victorian patriarchs.

2 SELF-RESPECT

At the heart of self-help, for Smiles, is the concept of self-respect: *'Self-respect is the noblest garment with which a man may clothe himself – the most elevating feeling with which the mind can be inspired.'*

DEFINING IDEA...

The pious and just honouring of ourselves may be thought the radical moisture and fountain-head from whence every laudable and worthy enterprise issues forth.

~ MILTON

Low self-esteem is often seen as something of a modern affliction – a staple of confessional chat-shows through which underachievers can sagely confide that their woes reside solely in the fact that they don't love themselves enough. Smiles might have had other words to add about why people fail to achieve but he certainly agreed that poor self-esteem can only hold us back and that conversely self-respect is the stepping-stone to greatness.

'Want of confidence is perhaps a greater obstacle to improvement than is generally imagined. It has been said that half the failures in life arise from pulling in one's horse while he is leaping.' He also noted that as well as being directly hamstrung by a lack of confidence, people are further handicapped since their lack of self-esteem has a knock-on effect on those around them: *'To think meanly of one's self, is to sink in one's own estimation as well as in the estimation of others.'* So, fail to respect yourself and you will fail to inspire respect from others – that much is as true today as it was in Smiles' time.

The problem, then, is learning to respect your own qualities. Here there's quite a major gap between Smiles' philosophy and the 'group hug' mentality of today's support groups. Smiles was more of a 'tough love' kind of guy and felt that too much guidance and help from others was like giving a life-jacket to a non-swimmer – it might keep them afloat, but it doesn't teach them to swim for themselves.

Nor would Smiles have taken to all those self-help gurus who advocate finding a success mantra and regularly telling your reflection how much you love yourself. In fact he felt the idea of trying to shore up self-esteem as a means of achieving success is likely to be counter-productive. *'One way in which self-culture may be degraded is by regarding it too exclusively as a means of 'getting on',* notes Smiles. Instead, he felt the way to grow self-respect was to apply yourself to your chosen task more energetically, with both head and hands, thereby becoming *'conscious of increasing power – perhaps the most cheering consciousness the human mind can cherish.'*

HERE'S AN IDEA FOR YOU...

Last thing after each working day, go over what you did and pick out five things you feel you did well. Give yourself a mental pat on the back but, more importantly, think what skills you brought to bear and how you could improve on the use of those skills next time.

3 SELF-DENIAL

Alongside self-respect, Smiles counted self-denial as a key step to independence, and yet one of the least popular. *'The lesson of self-denial – the sacrificing of a present gratification for a future good – is one of the last that is learnt.'*

Self-denial is a tough sell. It's precisely as tough to sell now as it was in Victorian times when Smiles said *'it must be admitted that 'self-denial and self-help' would make a poor rallying cry'*. The problem is that we all want a little reward for our daily struggles and some comfort when they seem to overcome us rather than the other way around.

DEFINING IDEA...

You may rely upon it that the Government of this country durst not tax the working classes to anything like the extent to which they tax themselves in their expenditure upon intoxicating drinks alone!

– LORD JOHN RUSSELL

The trouble with this is that sometimes the rewards become part of the problem. Take that doughnut you deserve after a gym session, or those doubles with soda to help you unwind after a hard day at the office – they're great at the time, but the calories condemn you to another gym session and the doubles set you off to face another tough day with a stressful hangover.

Smiles wasn't worried about waistlines or stress levels. He saw self-denial as the key to independence: *'The patriotism of this day has but little regard for such common things as individual economy and providence, although it is by the practice of such virtues only that the genuine independence of the industrial classes is to be secured.'* Dependency, be it a sweet little indulgence or a full-blown addiction, is more than just a bad habit in Smiles' eyes – it is enslavement in miniature. Only by being stronger than the habit can we go on to reform and optimise ourselves in other ways.

Partly this is a question of moral strength and willpower (as any smoker will have already noted) but Smiles also makes the point that many indulgences are a result of living short term. Of workers he notes that: *'The readiness with which so many are accustomed to eat up and drink up their earnings as they go renders them to a great extent helpless.'* His point is that self-denial is inextricably linked to seeing a bigger picture and planning for the future, both of which he sees as essential qualities on the path to greatness.

That mid-afternoon chocolate bar may seem like a harmless little treat, but if you are starting to count on it to get you through the day then you have created a dependency – a habit that is consuming you rather than the other way round.

HERE'S AN IDEA FOR YOU...

Small dependencies are often acceptable because we see them in isolation. Instead of thinking of the cost of that one 'for the road', calculate how many of those you buy in a year and what that annual cost to you is. Is there honestly nothing else more important you need that money for?

8

4 ON THE IMPORTANCE OF PLANNING

Financial planning may sound stuffy and dull, but for Smiles it is more than just a means of ensuring next year's holiday. Citing a Mr Cobden, he opines that *'The accomplishment of all other great works which have rendered man civilized and happy has been done by the savers, the thrifty; and those who have wasted their resources have always been their slaves.'*

DEFINING IDEA...

Never treat money affairs with levity. Money is character.

– SIR E. L. BULWER LYTTON, 19TH CENTURY ENGLISH WRITER

Sadly, this doesn't actually mean we belong in the 'great works' category just because we've got a tenner in a Post Office savings account. Instead, Smiles' point about financial planning is that a lack of it, much like a lack of self-denial, means that we are not truly in control of our lives. Smiles derided the devil-may-care lifestyle because he felt that it meant being entirely at the mercy of external factors and other people.

Taking control of your own destiny, for Smiles, is the mark of a man (and probably a woman too, though he never dwelt much on that). *'Any class of men that lives from hand to mouth will ever be an inferior class. They will necessarily remain impotent and helpless, hanging on to the skirts of society, the sport of times and seasons.'* This approach also ties in with his belief that self-respect lies at the heart of self-help – Smiles' view was that people who fail to plan their finances, and thereby leave their fortunes in the hands of others, show an essential lack of self-respect. In turn, that is likely to encourage a lack of respect from other people: *'Having no respect for themselves, they will fail in securing the respect of others.'*

Smiles uses the term 'slavery' again to describe the financially uncertain: *'The man who is always hovering on the verge of want is in a state not far removed from that of slavery. He is in no sense his own master.'*

When I was younger I laughed at the word 'pension' and dismissed any discussion of pensions as being dull stuff. Then someone pointed out that no matter how uncool pensions seemed to be, not having one was even less cool. It was then that I understood the point Smiles makes so forcefully. Happy-go-lucky is a romantic, cheery notion but underlying it is a failure to take responsibility for yourself. This, as Smiles points out, means that you are not truly your own master (or mistress) – which is not such a romantic, cheery notion.

HERE'S AN IDEA FOR YOU...

Most of us hesitate to put money to one side, so don't – let the bank do it. Open a savings account with a decent interest rate and instant access and set up a direct debit to pay into it every month. If at your year's end you haven't had to raid it, then transfer that sum to a long-term account with a better rate.

5 ECONOMISE AND THRIVE

'Better to look after petty savings than to descend to petty gettings,' says Smiles, meaning that small savings can make all the difference – even saving you the humiliation of doing work you feel is beneath your abilities. *'Every man ought so to contrive as to live within his means.'*

DEFINING IDEA...
We must carry money in the head, not in the heart.
~ JONATHAN SWIFT

Even in Victorian England, this was not a new statement but it was one to which Smiles added his own moral slant: *'This practice is the very essence of honesty. For if a man do not manage honestly to live within his own means, he must necessarily be living dishonestly upon the means of somebody else.'* He's saying that failing to live within your means isn't just about blowing more than you meant to this month on bananas and carpet cleaner, it's a moral issue, a failing, a question of honesty towards others as well as yourself.

Smiles advocates economy not because he has any great respect for money itself (he repeatedly says the importance of money is over-rated), but because he sees it as an imposition of order on to the potential chaos of daily life. *'Economy requires neither superior courage nor eminent virtue; it is satisfied with ordinary energy, and the capacity of average minds. Economy, at bottom, is but the spirit of order applied in the administration of domestic affairs: it means management regularity, prudence and the avoidance of waste.'*

Oddly enough those simple virtues of order, economy, and the avoidance of waste have just become a political issue in the UK, where Prime Minister Gordon Brown, faced with a recession and a global credit crunch, has highlighted the amount of food wasted by the average household. It may seem a mere distraction at a time when banks are themselves going bankrupt, but he has a good point. While most of us worry about reduced spending power we don't notice the money thrown in the bin every day. Official figures estimate that the typical household throws away £8 of unused food a week. That's £416 a year . . . in the bin.

Smiles would have been behind Brown all the way. Economy in this case is a classic case of imposing order and avoiding waste. It doesn't require some superhuman power or virtue; it is a very simple process and the savings would go directly into our own pocket but instead, through poor planning and purchasing, we blow the equivalent of a one-week package holiday every year. Petty savings can sometimes be so simple and so easy to put into practice that we overlook them altogether even though, seen in the long term, they can make a real difference to your lifestyle.

HERE'S AN IDEA FOR YOU...

Don't wait for the axe to fall. Imagine that recession means you have to cut 10% of the costs of your department/business without letting anyone go. Plan how you would do it and see if some of the options are worth implementing right now anyway. Get your colleagues to do the same.

6 BE TRUE TO YOURSELF

Given that he saw economy as a question of honesty, it is hardly surprising that Smiles saw debt in the same light: *'It is also difficult for a man who is in debt to be truthful; hence it is said that lying rides on debt's back.'* Make sure you're not already lying to yourself.

Smiles argued that debt and dishonesty went hand in hand because *'the debtor has to frame excuses to his creditor for postponing payment of the money he owes him; and probably also to contrive falsehoods.'* In the modern world, where debt is both much easier to acquire and less personal (few of us have had to lie to a credit card company about late payment), his point is still valid but mostly because we end up quietly lying to ourselves.

DEFINING IDEA...

Do not accustom yourself to consider debt only as an inconvenience; you will find it a calamity.

~ DR JOHNSON

Be honest: do you know exactly how much debt you have on credit cards, store cards, overdrafts, mortgages, personal loans, and mobile phone contracts (if you're not pay-as-you-go then you are borrowing as you go)? Do you really know the APR on each of these? Chances are you have a rough idea but you certainly don't add up the total. Debt has become a far more acceptable feature of daily life now than it was in Smiles' day – so much so that someone without credit cards and a mortgage is seen as a bit weird – even suspicious.

The temptation to ignore debt is as strong as it ever was and once again for Smiles this involves a strong moral element: *'It is the bounden duty of every man to look his affairs in the face,'* as he puts it. Smiles' argument was that you can't expect to go on to achieve greatness without first putting your own house in order. Much as with the issue of economy, he saw this as imposing order on immoral chaos.

This is good advice for individuals and companies alike, not least since banks and other lenders can rely on our self-imposed debt blindness to regularly raise interest rates without us raising any accompanying fuss. Whatever rate you were offered when you first took out that credit card, you can be sure that it has risen since. Although your bank most certainly sent you an explanatory letter, the chances are you barely glanced at it before getting on with something, anything, less unsavoury. Time to dig it out again and do your 'bounden duty' before that debt blindness comes back to bite you in the behind.

HERE'S AN IDEA FOR YOU...

Conduct a debt audit. List everything you owe and the interest rate you pay on it. You may be surprised by the rate on store cards in particular so transfer high-rate debts onto lower-rate cards or take an overdraft to pay them off (which is usually much cheaper debt). As soon as you have paid off a card, cut it up.

7 DO SWEAT THE SMALL STUFF

As well as being your bounden duty to look your affairs in the face, Smiles also insists that it is everyone's duty *'to keep an account of his incomings and outgoings in money matters'*. Take care of the pennies and the pounds/dollars/zloty will take care of themselves.

The problem with counting the pennies is that it is so often associated with the idea of Scrooge-like meanness. Attention to small detail is also often seen as the sign of a petty mind. Perhaps that's why Smiles chooses to illustrate the point with the stories of two men who are unlikely ever to be thought of as petty.

DEFINING IDEA...

Nothing is likelier to keep a man within compass than having constantly before his eyes the state of his affairs in a regular course of account.

~ JOHN LOCKE, PHILOSOPHER

He tells the story of the Duke of Wellington who *'kept an accurate detailed account of all the monies received and expended by him'*, a practice he learnt after having previously left a member of his staff to settle his accounts. He found out that the servant had been speculating with his money and that some of the bills had gone unpaid. Oddly enough that's pretty much what banks do whenever we pay in a cheque or wait for our money to be transferred from one account to another. It doesn't take four working days for an electronic transfer but the banks like to keep us waiting while they play with our funds. Wellington sacked his servant. We pay our banks for the same service.

George Washington likewise kept an eagle eye on all of his spending: *'he did not disdain to scrutinize even the smallest outgoings of his household – determined as he was to live honestly within his means – even while holding the high office of the President of the American Union.'*

Good accounting is the building block for any business whether self-employed or multinational and yet a surprising number of sharp-eyed businesspeople who would never allow waste or unaccounted-for expenditure in their companies don't give the slightest thought to their personal or household spending. In fact, as cash is increasingly replaced by debit cards, it has never been easier to keep track because all these electronic transactions leave a clear audit trail.

If you don't already use Internet banking then now's the time to start, given that it allows you a clear view across any number of accounts at any time of the month. There's no waiting for periodic statements to be sent out. Of course, though, online banking only makes sense if you then take the time to study your statements. So, get in the habit of logging on at the beginning and end of each week to see exactly where your hard-earned money is going.

HERE'S AN IDEA FOR YOU...

You've had to present your figures for personal, departmental, or corporate expenses to your company; why not to yourself? Break down your expenses under the headings of transport, clothing, utilities, entertainment, etc. and try presenting yourself with your quarterly financials. You are your own business – be a lean and mean one.

8 SOD THE JONESES

Long before there were BMWs, satellite dishes, or even net curtains through which to peer at them, there was the problem of keeping up with the Joneses: *'There is a dreadful ambition abroad for being "genteel". We keep up appearances, too often at the expense of honesty; and, though we may not be rich, yet we must seem to be so.'*

DEFINING IDEA...

My richness consisted not in the greatness of my possessions, but in the smallness of my wants.

~ EPITAPH OF JOSEPH BROTHERTON, POLITICIAN

Keeping up appearances, for Smiles, is another form of personal dishonesty and even cowardice, a point he illustrates with the story of Sir Charles Napier, chief of the army in India. Napier took steps to rein in the 'fast life' being led by so many of his young officers. He maintained that *"to drink unpaid-for champagne and unpaid-for beer, and to ride unpaid-for horses, is to be a cheat, and not a gentleman."*

More than that, Napier noted that he had many *"gallant young fellows . . . capable of mounting a breach on an emergency amidst belching fire, and of performing the most desperate deeds of valour, who nevertheless cannot or will not exercise the moral courage necessary to enable them to resist a petty temptation presented to their senses. They cannot utter their valiant 'No' or 'I can't afford it'."* In short, these young officers were happier to face gory death than to face the ridicule of their peers.

These days most of us would probably opt not to drive this year's model rather than die bloodily on a Baluchi battlefield but there's still an element of truth in the observation. Even if we're not conscious of the ridicule behind not keeping up appearances, we still suffer from the syndrome in an insidious way. The personal arms-race of keeping up is founded on an insecurity; the idea that we are not complete unless we compete materially with our peers. The sad thing is that this means we often take on aspirations that are not strictly our own. People who never noticed what this year's model looked like suddenly hanker after one because the neighbour has one. Their aspiration becomes ours.

Celebrity magazines are stuffed with the minutiae of the lives and possessions of the famous so we then aspire to be like them, even when those possessions are in all probability product placements by manufacturers keen to kindle our envy. Don't be taken in – the best way to keep up with anybody is to be happier than they are, and that's not so easily bought. The only people who really find solace in retail therapy are the companies selling the stuff. For the rest of us, consumerism is a very short-term solution with a longer term financial hangover. If we really needed all the stuff we're being sold, why would companies have to spend fortunes on advertising?

HERE'S AN IDEA FOR YOU...

Take a step back and break down your actions. When you sense that you are stretching out for an aspirational goal, analyse it carefully to see if it is really yours, or whether you are in the process of inheriting someone else's dream just to keep up. Then ask if you really want to define personal success by taking on the insecurities of others.

9 UNEMPLOYMENT, SICKNESS AND DEATH

Smiles observes: *'When a man casts his glance forward, he will find that the three chief temporal contingencies for which he has to provide are want of employment, sickness and death. The two first he may escape, but the last is inevitable.'*

DEFINING IDEA...

In this world nothing can be said to be certain, except death and taxes.

~ BENJAMIN FRANKLIN

Smiles was way ahead of his time in this since the idea of insurance and assurance were nowhere near as well established as they are now. Nonetheless he is clear about what has to be done about it and his advice is much the same as any insurance company would give today about thinking about the unthinkable. *'It is . . . the duty of the prudent man so to live, and so to arrange, that the pressure of suffering, in event of either contingency occurring, shall be mitigated to as great an extent as possible, not only to himself, but also to those who are dependent upon him for their comfort and subsistence.'*

Given the limited range of financial services available at the time, Smiles didn't propose unemployment cover but instead suggested that everyone try to build up a savings bulwark – a lump sum to act as a buffer in case sickness or unemployment stopped them from earning at any point.

Today there are a number of options available. Yes, you can still put aside a lump sum (preferably in a high-interest rate account) but to do that you first have to have that disposable wealth. Alternatively you can take out insurance. A lot of us make the mistake of thinking that national health schemes will pay for any medical problems that arise but that mistake is usually revealed the first time you need some dental work. Taking out private medical cover will help you jump queues and get preventative work done on such things as latent sports injuries that normal national schemes may not cover.

But that's only the start. Consider not just the cost of the medical care but any impact on your earnings. A broken arm could mean months off the job if you do manual work. What happens then? Full protection also means unemployment coverage for credit cards and debts which pays off the interest when you can't. It might also mean the ability to take a payment holiday on the mortgage to take the pressure off your finances for a couple of months while you recuperate or find a new job if you're made redundant.

As for the big final pay off, you should leave at least enough money for your funeral, but if you have family who count on your income then life assurance is a must. You'll have to assess your personal risk by taking into account your job security, health risks and dependants but a good insurance broker will be happy to help.

HERE'S AN IDEA FOR YOU...

Check out the increasingly popular 'medical tourism' packages, where you fly to another part of the world with cheaper health care, have your teeth/knee/hip sorted out privately for a fraction of the cost back home, and enjoy a few days in the sun to sweeten the pill.

10 BE BIGGER THAN THE BUSINESS

A great believer in applying yourself to the job at hand, Smiles was nonetheless keen to point out the importance of not getting bogged down in the dull details of the daily grind. *'A youth may handle a yardstick, or measure a piece of ribbon; and there will be no discredit in doing so, unless he allows his mind to have no higher range than the stick and ribbon; to be as short as the one, and as narrow as the other.'*

We've all met them; those insufferable bores who drone on interminably about the minutiae of their job because there is simply nothing else going on in their heads. If they happened to be doing a stint leading the UN or single-handedly running the World Health Organisation, it would be forgivable, but the drones in question are without exception doing some of the dullest jobs known to man.

DEFINING IDEA...

We are all of us in the gutter, but some of us are looking at the stars.
~ OSCAR WILDE

Perhaps boring the rest of us is their revenge on society. More likely, the chances are that they have simply failed to look for the big picture and identify not only how to do that work, but where that work is taking them. Nor can the blame for that be laid at the door of the job itself – it's not the fact of doing a dull job that makes a dull person. It is down to the individual to make more of themselves and not be defined by something as petty and arbitrary as a job title. Smiles gives the example of Flechier, Bishop of Nimes, who had started out life as a candle maker and was taunted for it by a doctor. *"If you had been born in the same condition that I was,"* replied the Bishop, *"you would still have been but a maker of candles."*

Smiles sees honour in every job well done, but the point is that lowly jobs don't have to mean low expectations. Greatness comes to those who can see the relative lowness of the job at hand but still get on with it while all the time looking for the next step forwards. Failing to do a job because you believe it is beneath you or becoming obsessed with a job and not looking beyond it are the twin evils that stop us achieving our potential. The problem is that it is all too easy to allow work to fill our horizons and blot out the sun in the process – all the more so if we spend a lot of our free time socialising with colleagues or people in the same line of business.

HERE'S AN IDEA FOR YOU...

Stalin wasn't the only fan of five-year plans and they don't have to involve tractor-making or gulags. Think about where you want to be five years from now, including role, job title, earnings, or a total change of field. Now work out what you aim for each year on the way to getting there.

11 GET OUT OF THE RUT

As well as the attitude of not looking beyond business, Smiles warned of the habit of getting into a rut at work. *'The business man gets into a rut, and often does not look beyond it. If he lives for himself only, he becomes apt to regard other human beings only in so far as they minister to his ends.'*

DEFINING IDEA...

The difference between a rut and a grave is the depth.

~ GERALD BURRILL, RETIRED EPISCOPAL BISHOP OF CHICAGO

Smiles illustrates the rut of business by comparing it to a monkey trapped by a treat placed within a hollow gourd. The monkey reaches in through a hole in the gourd and grabs the treat but because its clenched fist is now bigger than the hole, it is trapped. As long as the monkey refuses to let go of the spoils, it is itself a prisoner.

The lesson is that for as long as we focus too much on material gains, we are trapped by our own greed. Despite Smiles' emphasis on the value of hard work, he is not overly impressed by the acquisition of wealth for its own sake. The answer, he suggests, is to take the time to consider our fellow man, and not as a mere agent for our own progress. Ideally the application of this would be to trot off and find a cure for cancer or set up a hospital for incurables. However, full-on philanthropy of that sort is not a reasonable route for many of us, even though Smiles gives us a fair few examples of people who have made that journey. You don't actually have to go and work with refugees in Chad in order to shift your focus from yourself. Simple awareness of others is a first step to escaping that rut, not to mention getting your hairy little fist out of that gourd.

Meeting with other minds is a great way of putting your own life in perspective and finding or fine-tuning your goals and aspirations. If you could invite Richard Branson, Nelson Mandela, Bill Gates, and Anita Roddick around for supper it would give you an excellent insight into a rich vein of goals and ideas on how to achieve them. If you don't have their numbers on speed dial, however, then reading the biographies of those you admire is another means of meeting other minds and comparing your own aims and progress with theirs.

The rich and famous don't have a monopoly on aspiration, however, so stop going for coffee or drinks with your colleagues and spend a little more time talking to people from other walks of life.

HERE'S AN IDEA FOR YOU...

Pick a hero/heroine. It could be a business mogul, a spiritual leader, or a sportsman, but choose someone who inspires you. Don't focus on their achievements but instead on the attitudes and attributes that got them there. Now try to look at your life through their eyes and think how they would improve it.

12 GETTING PARTNERS ON BOARD

Women don't figure much in *Self-help*. Of those that do, at least one – referred to only as Arkwright's wife – is seen as a bit of a hindrance. *'His wife . . . was impatient at what she conceived to be a wanton waste of time and money, and in a moment of sudden wrath she seized upon and destroyed his models.'* In reality there is a lot to learn from Arkwright and his wife.

The models Arkwright's wife destroyed were the prototypes of the spinning machine that would eventually revolutionise the industry, create the modern factory system, and lead to Arkwright becoming High Sheriff of Derbyshire and being knighted. Arkwright's wife didn't get to share in that success since they separated immediately after the incident of the model wrecking.

DEFINING IDEA...

It is probably not love that makes the world go around, but rather those mutually supportive alliances through which partners recognise their dependence on each other for the achievement of shared and private goals.
~ FRED ALLEN, AMERICAN COMEDIAN

Although Smiles doesn't judge the wife or reflect much on her outburst, he does mention that she did it *'hoping thus to remove the cause of the family privations'* – meaning that Arkwright's single-minded pursuit of his goal was interfering with his ability to provide his family and rather than see the machine as a way out of their difficulties she saw it as the cause of them.

To modern management this represents a clear failure to communicate. If Arkwright's wife had shared his vision she would never have smashed the models, so it seems reasonable to conclude that either he hadn't shared it with her or he hadn't convinced her sufficiently of its worth.

Victorian attitudes to sexual equality were a little basic so it's entirely possible that the founding of the factory system wasn't considered a suitable subject for the unnamed wife but that's not an acceptable attitude in this day and age. If you want to achieve greatness and elevate your life to match your dreams, then your personal partner is more than a fellow traveller; he or she is your wingman, watching your back and clearing the way for you to make your approach.

Having developed a goal and dared to dream you now have to share it with your nearest and dearest – indeed, sell it to them – so that you can shoot for it with their support. Trying to go it alone or jealously hiding your aims is only going to generate a climate of alienation and mistrust. If you don't dare to declare your dream to the most important person in your life then it's time to ask yourself which one you don't have faith in – the plan or the partner.

HERE'S AN IDEA FOR YOU...

Deliver a presentation to your loved one(s). Call it a rehearsal for a work presentation and say how much you value their feedback while taking the opportunity to present your ideas as you would to a potential investor. They will be more likely to buy in to what you're doing and you may be surprised by their perspectives.

13 STRENGTH AND STRENGTH OF CHARACTER

'There are many tests by which a gentleman may be known; but there is one that never fails – how does he exercise power over those subordinate to him?' For 'gentleman' read 'good manager'.

DEFINING IDEA...

It is excellent to have a giant's strength; but it is tyrannous to use it like a giant.

~ WILLIAM SHAKESPEARE, MEASURE FOR MEASURE

Having established that the way out of a rut is to pay more attention to our fellow man, Smiles goes on to assert that the real mark of a strong person is how gently they treat others. Actually, he blows it a bit for the modern reader by ranking women as 'subordinates' but he was writing in an era when a large number of top professions were closed to women and little attention was paid to the women earning livings in the professions that remained.

Leaving aside the issue of sexism, Smiles' advice is as good for the modern manager as it was for the Victorian gentleman: *'A consideration for the feelings of others, for his inferiors and dependants as well as his equals, and respect for their self-respect, will pervade the true gentleman's whole conduct.'* The great man or woman is not the one who shouts loudest or bullies those beneath them, although a mixture of bad managers and media stereotypes means that the bullying approach is still tolerated in business. There is probably a whole generation of managers in the making who think that leadership is the style affected by Alan Sugar or Donald Trump in *The Apprentice*. That kind of behaviour is a mark of insecurity, or as Smiles rather neatly puts it: *'The tyrant . . . is but a slave turned inside out.'*

Instead the manager with true strength of character can afford to be considerate and even *'rather himself suffer a small injury, than by an uncharitable construction of another's behaviour, incur the risk of committing a great wrong'*. In other words, they give the benefit of the doubt to dubious behaviour rather than wade in and rail at someone only to find out they meant nothing wrong.

Good managers succeed because of, not in spite of, their teams and raise their game by raising the game of the whole team, not by distancing themselves from them in pointing out their errors. There's a simple test to see if you show true strength, as seen by Smiles, and that's to ask yourself how open you are to input from junior colleagues. If people come to you with suggestions of different ways to do things, you're probably open and approachable. If they don't, then instead of blaming them for being lumpen, ask yourself if there isn't a hint of the tyrant in the way you work.

HERE'S AN IDEA FOR YOU...

Worked out your five-year plan to personal glory? Great. Now it's time to do the same for your employees. Sit them down and talk to them about what they want and how they see themselves getting it. Helping them advance their careers could well be the key to advancing your own.

14 DO YOUR RESEARCH

"I will defend you to the best of my ability," says the lawyer Sir
John Copley to his client John Heathcoat. As Smiles points
out, Sir John's ability proved itself as he went the extra mile
in learning about the business in hand.

DEFINING IDEA...

Knowledge is of two kinds:
we know a subject ourselves,
or we know where we can
find information upon it.
~ SAMUEL JOHNSON

John Heathcoat invented the bobbin-net
machine, a *'mechanical pillow for making
lace'*, which involved a fiendishly complicated
mechanism that twisted and tied threads to
create lace. When he finally got his prototype
to work, he took the precaution of patenting
it. This was a time of unprecedented activity in the field of inventing
manufacturing machines and patents were hard to protect. Parallel
inventions and plagiarism both led to conflicting claims, so much so that
when one lace manufacturer took another to court for an infringement of
his copyright the judge ruled they were both in infringement of Heathcoat's
patent.

Heathcoat found himself in court to protect his intellectual property and
his lawyer was Sir John Copley. We should all have a Sir John in our corner.
Not only did he lock himself away with the machine until he understood
its workings, he also wouldn't leave it until he had learnt how to make lace
himself. When it came to his day in court he understood his subject so well
that he was able to make his point clear to judge, jury, and spectators alike.
Heathcoat and Copley won the case and *'after the trial was over, Mr Heathcoat,*

on inquiry, found about six hundred machines at work after his patent, and he proceeded to levy royalty upon the owners of them, which amounted to a large sum.' Heathcoat was a made man, in no small part thanks to Copley's approach to his job, which consisted of learning his client's business to such a degree of detail that he was able to do it himself.

The lesson here is that rather than rely on his established legal knowledge or have Heathcoat (the expert) explain to him, Copley opted to approach the problem as a complete newcomer and engage with it so completely that he would understand not only the theory but also the practice of the business. You don't have to be a consultant to see the value in that (though if you are a consultant you might want to make notes). There's a line of thinking that says you don't need to understand every aspect of your business – as long as you have experts on hand who know their speciality. Yet Copley showed that going the extra mile and getting to grips with the detail can pay off handsomely.

HERE'S AN IDEA FOR YOU...

Ever been told your business can't do something because of technology/ logistics/machinery? Did you ask why and force yourself to truly understand the reason? Or did you ask and then glaze over as the answer was given? From now on, lock yourself in the room with business conundrums until you know them so well that you can see solutions.

15 BEWARE THE LUDDITES

'Machine breakers organized themselves in regular bodies, and held nocturnal meetings at which their plans were arranged. Probably with the view of inspiring confidence, they gave out that they were under the command of a leader named Ned Ludd, or General Ludd, and hence their designation of Luddites.' **Ned Ludd may be long gone, but his legacy remains.**

DEFINING IDEA...

Criticism is not nearly as effective as sabotage.

~ TRADITIONAL WORKPLACE HUMOUR

People jokingly call themselves Luddites when they struggle with computers, forgetting perhaps that Luddites weren't slow adopters; they were vicious saboteurs who murdered mill bosses. Modern Luddites don't usually lynch members of the IT department (however tempted) and rarely smash their machines but they do, and will, sabotage your projects and innovations through silent resistance.

It doesn't have to be about technology, either: new systems, processes, or attitudes are all it takes to put some people's backs up and have them silently dig in ready for the long, slow, siege of the 'over my dead body' brigade. Worse, they don't always show their resistance, but instead appear to accept the new while conducting conspiratorial chats around the coffee machine and gently poisoning their peers with gripes and grudges.

In England, the Luddites were broken by the force of the law and the threat of the noose. However, no matter how appealing that may sound in your workplace, it's not likely to be a tactic open to you. Smiles looks across the

Channel to tell the tale of Jacquard and his loom, which so upset the good folk of Lyons that they tried to drown him. He was rescued, however, in part by the English, since they happily adopted the loom. The workers of Lyons then had the sense to see that if they didn't do likewise, those ghastly rosbifs were going to do them out of a job. *'Then it was, and only then, that Lyons, threatened to be beaten out of the field, adopted it with eagerness; and before long the Jacquard machine was employed in nearly all kinds of weaving.'*

Jacquard was lucky – he had an external threat on hand that his workers could understand and that helped him implement his changes. Changes in business shouldn't be inspired by a whim but instead by either a threat or opportunity so in theory there is no reason not to explain that to those involved. After all, if you don't think the arguments in favour of the change are particularly convincing then perhaps you should consider if the change is worthwhile. If you don't think the change is worthwhile, or think it is being foisted on you, then don't forget that you too are a potential Luddite and ask for more support from above.

HERE'S AN IDEA FOR YOU...

Make people share in a change. Invite them to help draft it and allocate roles for implementing it. Clearly identify their areas of responsibility. Inclusion goes a long way towards overcoming resistance and clear demarcation of responsibility helps deal with the effects of reluctance when they happen.

16 A TREASURE TROVE OF WISDOM

While constantly applauding personal application and industry, Smiles also notes the external factors that contribute to greatness. In the case of Jacquard and his loom, Smiles highlights the importance of his time in the Conservatoire, *'where he had the advantage of minutely inspecting the various exquisite pieces of mechanism contained in that great treasury of human ingenuity.'*

DEFINING IDEA...

The doorstep to the temple of wisdom is a knowledge of our own ignorance.

– BENJAMIN FRANKLIN

In a time of frenzied innovation it is all the more important not to waste time reinventing the wheel – a message as true in the 21st century as it was in the 1800s. The Conservatoire des Arts et Métiers in Paris was, and still is, a museum of inventions and prototypes from all fields of engineering and industry. It's probably now most famous as the home of Foucault's pendulum. Jacquard, busily working on his loom design, sufficiently impressed the Emperor to be allowed to use its workshop and there he took the opportunity to study a silk loom invented by Vaucanson. Studying the details of that earlier invention *"set him upon the track of his discovery"*.

In effect, the Conservatoire served as a repository of knowledge, carefully indexed and very detailed. Dipping into it saved Jacquard many years of development time. The problem in modern business is that knowledge is often much more ephemeral and scattered. Companies don't know how much they know and usually don't realise that until some individual – a salesperson with an intimate knowledge of customers and prospects, for example – leaves. As long as accrued wisdom is stored only in the minds (and Post-it notes) of the individuals doing the learning, it is very hard for the business to profit from it and to make the next step forward when the time comes to innovate.

The answer has to be a shared pool of information – the goal of modern knowledge management. That means more than a central database of contact and product information, which should already be stored and accessible. Those kinds of facts are only a small part of the picture, however. A good knowledge pool, typically held on a company-wide intranet, will also include winning presentations, notes about the particularities of demanding clients, tips on regional differences, customer feedback, and even (rarest and most valuable of all) examples and details of major mistakes so they can be avoided in future. A really good intranet – such as Truffles, the in-house repository of advertising giant Ogilvy – includes training materials and strategy structures so the next time a client asks you to implement something you've never heard of, at least you know where to start.

HERE'S AN IDEA FOR YOU...

Knowledge is power, and people naturally hoard both. It's therefore vital to offer an incentive to encourage people to share. Make your intranet enjoyable and try a ratings system whereby the more people contribute, the higher they are ranked, until they reach expert level. Then pay them. Reward and recognition go a long way to fostering a culture of sharing.

17 BURNING DOWN THE HOUSE

'A life distinguished for heroic labour, extraordinary
endurance, inflexible rectitude, and the exhibition of many
rare and noble virtues' – such is Smiles' verdict on Bernard
Palissy, a man whose single-minded perseverance in the
face of setbacks verged on the insane (and some would say
crossed the line).

DEFINING IDEA...

*Life takes on meaning when
you become motivated, set
goals and charge after them
in an unstoppable manner.*

~ LES BROWN, US AUTHOR,
ENTREPRENEUR AND MOTIVATOR

There's no shortage of examples of successful
businessmen who have stuck at it despite
setbacks and achieved their goal, but there can't
be many like Bernard Palissy. Having been
inspired by a single Italian cup, he set his mind
to creating enamel – to thereby lift pottery to
a finer art form. The problem was that he had
no idea how it was made and so he was starting from scratch. The rest of us
would have got help or given up at this point, and with good reason, but
Palissy proceeded to spend the following sixteen years experimenting with
different kilns, materials and mixes.

The turning point for Palissy came when, out of a batch of 300 pieces of
pottery, he found a single one that had turned out with a fine glaze of white
enamel. Three hundred to one seemed like reasonable odds to him and so he
kept at it with a determination bordering on obsessive compulsive. On one
occasion when his kiln had reached a crucial stage, he realised it was running
out of fuel. Ripping up all the fence posts from the garden, he recharged the

fire, but even then it wasn't enough and the glaze refused to form. Looking around, there was no other source of wood – except one …

'There remained the household furniture and shelving. A crashing noise was heard in the house; and amidst the screams of his wife and children, who now feared Palissy's reason was giving way, the tables were seized, broken up and heaved into the furnace.' Palissy threw it all into the flames in his attempt to get the enamel to form while his wife and children ran from the house screaming that he had gone mad. He got there in the end and Palissy's enamel became sought-after by the great and good. Smiles doesn't relate how the rest of the family felt about it.

Refusal to give up is a hard lesson to take to heart, but the real point of Palissy's story was that having truly set your heart on a single goal there can be no going back. The art, therefore, is to make quite sure that if you set your sights on something, you'd be prepared to burn your furniture to get it.

HERE'S AN IDEA FOR YOU...

Palissy refused to sell the sub-standard work he made en route to his goal and so never debased his brand, which enhanced its value when he got the product right. Write down the likely compromises that will be asked of you on the way to your goal and decide now, before they arise, which ones you would be better off refusing to make in the long run.

18 IF YOU CAN'T MAKE GOLD, MAKE PORCELAIN

Frederick Böttgher was an enterprising man. Unusually amongst Smiles' heroes, he was also a complete crook. Claiming to have successfully turned base metal to gold he found himself threatened with the gallows as a fraud – until another alchemist, Walter von Tshirnhaus, suggested to him: "If you can't make gold, try something else; make porcelain."

DEFINING IDEA...

I find that a great part of the information I have was acquired by looking up something and finding something else on the way.

~ FRANKLIN P. JONES, US BUSINESSMAN, 1887–1929

Having initially, for whatever reason, claimed to have created gold from copper, Böttgher soon found himself the subject of unwanted attention as a number of people (presumably the ones with substantial stocks of copper) became very insistent that he repeat the feat. Since he'd never made gold in the first place this was going to prove tricky, to say the least. The advice from von Tshirnhaus was his salvation as he turned his knowledge of chemistry and the effects of heat to the art of transforming clay into fine porcelain. He succeeded and fired up the porcelain industry as a result.

However, this is not to say that you should go around claiming the ability to turn copper into gold – although there are a fair few management gurus who effectively do just that. The point is almost an alternative viewpoint to the story of Palissy in Idea 17. It's tempting to think that von Tshirnhaus and Böttgher both knew that their 'art' was fraudulent. But, even if they didn't, and they believed in their end goal, it was proving tough to reach and unlikely to be achieved by the deadline.

So, rather than work exclusively for an unattainable goal, von Tshirnhaus's idea was to take the learning and talent developed to date and use it to achieve waypoint goals – the worth of which would justify the original project. There are many modern examples of waypoint goals, such as the invention of Teflon as part of NASA's project to put a man on the moon. The World Wide Web was invented as a side effect of the CERN particle accelerator programme – originally conceived purely for scientists to trade notes, it certainly didn't damage the reputation or funding of Tim Berners Lee or CERN.

A waypoint goal doesn't have to be a product; it can be a way of working, a methodology or a better means of storing the findings of your main project. What it does mean is that paying particular attention to the steps on the way to the final goal can pay bonuses that help keep the entire project alive.

HERE'S AN IDEA FOR YOU...

Got a tough project in hand, or a very long-term goal? Without losing site of it, draw up four or five waypoint goals and decide not just what deliverables they entail but also what the value of those would be to which client (internal or external). Now sell those goals to protect the original objective and your reputation.

19 EXIT STRATEGIES

Instead of ruling the roost, the golden goose is just as likely to find itself enslaved. Once our friend Böttgher from Idea 18 started to deliver, he was basically imprisoned: *'[He was] under strict surveillance, for fear lest he should communicate his secret to others or escape the Elector's control. The new workshops and furnaces erected for him were guarded by troops night and day.'*

DEFINING IDEA...

Quitting is not an exit strategy.

~ DONALD RUMSFELD,
US SECRETARY OF DEFENSE

You have to suspect that any man who'd once claimed to make gold from copper was worth keeping an eye on but it wasn't until the one-time alchemist broke through as a genuine porcelain manufacturer that the he found himself really locked down. Essentially, Böttgher was imprisoned because he had made himself too valuable. As an alchemist he had always had a vested interest in keeping the tricks of his trade to himself and then, as a master of porcelain, it seems he did much the same. In one letter to the king he begs for his freedom but at the same time unwittingly argues against it: *"I will devote my whole soul to the art of making porcelain, I will do more than any inventor ever did before; only give me liberty, liberty!"*

The mistake here is the emphasis on himself – the 'I' of that letter. By pushing himself as the single and absolute key to the business, he ensured his own lock-in. Böttgher had little understanding of escape strategy.

Nowadays, we can similarly find ourselves trapped in jobs or roles simply because we become too proficient and the organisation has no incentive to find a replacement – fine if that's all you ever wanted to do, but a ball and chain if you want to move onwards and upwards. Even after he retired, a pensions specialist who worked for a global car rental company was still being called back in to help, which he continued to do despite grumbling and asking when the company was ever going to find a replacement. The answer, of course, was that they would start looking on the day he declined to do the job.

It's common to talk of exit strategies as if they only affected entrepreneurs selling off their self-made companies and cashing in. In truth we all need an exit strategy if we're ever going to go from one role to another. Take a tip from the exit experts: they don't just jump ship; they start by selling the idea that it will be beneficial to the organisation if there is a progressive hand-over to another party. They groom successors instead of jealously guarding secrets and, finally, when they move on they do so in such a way that anyone involved in old and new roles thanks them for it.

HERE'S AN IDEA FOR YOU...

Stop thinking it's good to be indispensable. The good manager hones his or her team to a point where it barely needs management at all. It may seem risky but you have to if you want to move to a new post. Decide what you contribute personally and decide a) how that could be replaced and b) why it would be best applied elsewhere.

20 PURE GENIUS

'The extraordinary results effected by dint of sheer industry and perseverance have led many distinguished men to doubt whether the gift of genius be so exceptional an endowment as it is usually supposed to be,' says Smiles. Perhaps genius is merely patience.

We're accustomed to thinking of genius as a wild and flashy attribute, an extraordinary, left-field approach to thinking. Smiles suggests that it may actually be within the grasp of many if not most of us. *'The very greatest men have been among the least believers in the power of genius ... some have even defined genius to be only common sense intensified.'* Elsewhere he adds that *'John Foster [preacher and essayist] held it to be the power of lighting one's own fire.'*

DEFINING IDEA...

...it is patience.

~ COMTE DE BUFFON, CELEBRATED
NATURALIST, DEFINING GENIUS

Smiles does, though, argue that *'it must nevertheless be sufficiently obvious that, without the original endowment of heart and brain, no amount of labour, however well applied, could have produced a Shakespeare, a Newton, a Beethoven, or a Michelangelo.'* Yet he also quotes a wide range of great men to suggest that true genius is rare, and the secret of more everyday genius is available to all of us. *'Locke, Helvetius, and Diderot believed that all men have an equal aptitude for genius and that what some are able to effect, under the laws of the intellect, must also be within the reach of others who, under like circumstances, apply themselves to like pursuits.'* That sounds like a very worthy, dry and, frankly, dull Victorian approach to the idea of genius: work hard enough, apply yourself with sufficient diligence and you will achieve greatness.

The pace of change has accelerated radically since Smiles' day and in order to make your mark in a world of information overload it is possible that a degree of eccentricity, colour, and even showmanship are expected of those we like to call genius. You could say that Smiles was talking of a time when inventions could take generations of work, and once in place would last for generations more before being superseded. Yet it is also possible that energy and application can still be all you need to rise above the common crowd. Richard Branson started by selling records above a shoe shop and he has in many ways applied a single consistent approach to business from the earliest days. What has made him a giant has been the energy with which he has brought that approach to bear across such a wide range of businesses. They haven't all succeeded (Virgin computers anyone?) but his tireless consistency has made him a household name and Virgin a global brand.

HERE'S AN IDEA FOR YOU...

Due diligence should mean more than part of the process of a business takeover. Get in the habit of looking at projects and identifying what is based on sure knowledge and what is based on assumptions. From now on, replace the risk of guesswork with the legwork of research to find figures or examples to fill the gaps.

21 GET HELP

'One morning Buffon was unusually obstinate, and Joseph found it necessary to resort to the extreme measure of dashing a basin of ice-cold water under the bed-clothes, the effect of which was instantaneous.' Sometimes, a helping hand can come as a bit of a shock to the system but, with the story of the Comte de Buffon, Smiles illustrates the motivation that can come from others.

DEFINING IDEA...

I get by with a little help from my friends.

~ JOHN LENNON

The Comte de Buffon went on to become a famous naturalist but referred to himself as having been an indolent youth (there's another kind?) and struggled with the temptation to lie in bed, thereby wasting hours every morning. The solution he came to was to charge his servant, Joseph, with the job of getting his distinguished derriére out from under the duvet each morning. *'He ... failed in being able to rise at the hour he had fixed. He then called his servant to his help, and promised him the reward of a crown every time that he succeeded in getting him up before six.'*

This proved tricky because Buffon, like most of us, tended to grumpiness on being woken up and so when Joseph first tried to get him out of bed he would pretend to be sick, or yell at him, or even threaten to fire him. Eventually, however, it seems that either Joseph stopped believing the threats, or really needed that crown, or simply decided that the comte had it coming to him and resorted to the ice water approach. Dramatic, but effective.

Smiles doesn't actually tell us if Joseph stuck with the shock approach, but whatever technique he developed it seems that he persisted and Buffon got out of the habit of staying in bed: *'By the persistent use of such means, Buffon at length conquered his habit; and he was accustomed to say that he owed to Joseph three or four volumes of his Natural History.'*

Ice water and servants don't tend to feature much in our lives but a lack of discipline surely does. You're that much more likely to make it to the gym on time if you have a personal trainer tapping his or her watch if you're late. Likewise, if you want to get into the habit of early morning runs then agreeing to meet another runner at a point some way from both of your homes is far more effective than relying on willpower alone to get out of a warm bed and into your running shoes.

HERE'S AN IDEA FOR YOU...

Learning a language? Preparing for an exam? Get a study partner. Agree to both attend the same class or meet for revision sessions at set times and for a set period. Now set a penalty if either of you fails to turn up. It should be a realistic penalty that's a little painful to part with if it's going to work well.

22 GETTING BACK ON THE HORSE

'Any man can do what any other man has done,' says Smiles, quoting Dr Young, the philosopher, and illustrating it with Young's dogged refusal to accept failure. I'm not sure we can all do what Neil Armstrong has done, but as a maxim in business it holds surprisingly true.

DEFINING IDEA...

My great concern is not whether you have failed, but whether you are content with your failure.

~ ABRAHAM LINCOLN

Dr Young first went riding with a well-known horseman who leapt a high fence on their first outing. Presumably he was showing off to the new boy, but if he was then he picked the wrong audience because the good doctor immediately tried to do the same thing. He fell off, unsurprisingly, but Smiles goes on to tell us that he wouldn't give up. *'Without saying a word, he remounted, made a second effort, and was again unsuccessful, but this time he was not thrown further than on to the horse's neck, to which he clung. At the third trial, he succeeded and cleared the fence.'*

Similarly Smiles tells the tale of a missionary called Carey who fell out of a tree he was climbing when a boy, breaking his leg in the process. *'He was confined to his bed for weeks, but when he recovered and was able to walk without support, the very first thing he did was to go and climb that tree.'* We all know the maxim of getting back on the horse that has thrown you, but don't always apply it to ourselves. In some cases a fear of failure stops us from even beginning to attempt something we perceive as difficult. Presentations leap to mind as an example. It might feel like dodging a bullet to get out of doing a presentation but in reality you've as good as fallen off the horse without even mounting it.

Cultural issues also play a part in the fear of failure and the response to it. In the UK, for example, it is still seen as shameful to have launched a business only for it to fail. In the US the failed businessperson is more likely to be seen as a good bet second time around since the presumption is that they have learned from the lesson and have the courage to get up, dust themselves off, and have another go. In professional training, I have often observed that those who struggle with a skill, but stick with it until they master it, often become better at it than the naturals who have never had to focus on overcoming a handicap. So, look that horse firmly in the eye and get back on it.

HERE'S AN IDEA FOR YOU...

Re-examine your failure, or fear of failure, and draw up everything you can learn from it. Then think about how to address each point in turn and see where external help could make you improve. Now use that combination of help and experience as your leg-up back into the saddle.

23 SEEING WITH THE MIND

'It is the mind that sees as well as the eye,' says Smiles, explaining that while there is a lot to be learnt by observing, the person who has already engaged with an issue or problem will see a lot more than someone who expects to learn by looking alone.

The story of Sir Isaac Newton 'discovering' gravity while observing an apple falling from the tree is such a familiar one that we don't question the basic flaw in it. Newton didn't just see an apple fall and go 'aha – gravity'. Instead, his mind had been continually churning theories of physics until the revealing observation clarified them.

DEFINING IDEA...

Our observation of nature must be diligent, our reflection profound, and our experiments exact. We rarely see these three means combined; and for this reason, creative geniuses are not common.
– DENIS DIDEROT, FRENCH PHILOSOPHER

'In like manner,' notes Smiles, *'the brilliantly coloured soap-bubbles blown from a common tobacco pipe – though "trifles light as air" in most eyes – suggested to Dr Young his beautiful theory of "interferences", and led to his discovery relating to the diffraction of light.'*

Smiles' point is that we accept a lot of discoveries as being 'accidental' when they clearly aren't. There may be tiny revelations that help put a theory or discovery into place but these revelations are usually visible to everyone, all of the time. There's no counting the number of people who had seen a soap bubble but not hit upon diffraction, or an apple fall without discovering gravity. Every single one of us has slipped thankfully into a bath, but we do so without a thought for the mass and volume of water we displace, far less the implications that has on whether or not any given object will float. When Archimedes had his 'eureka' moment it was merely a moment of clarity in an ongoing mental investigation.

Most of us observe phenomena continuously without dwelling on their causes or implications. The ones who have already brought their minds to bear on a subject are the ones who fully appreciate what they are looking at – like Galileo's understanding of a pendulum based on his observation of a swinging oil lamp.

In business and personal life, as in science, the vast majority of us sleepwalk through our daily lives observing but not necessarily absorbing the lessons around us. We think we are watching attentively but because we're staring at the results of things without dwelling on their implications we miss the true gravity (sorry) of what we're seeing. Because it's easier to observe the results of a problem than divine their cause, we often deal with business problems after the fact instead of proactively.

HERE'S AN IDEA FOR YOU...

Is that underperforming colleague lazy, or do they feel passed-over for promotion? Do staff avoid admin because it's complex, or because they need training? List your business problems and for each one come up with three causes other than the one you presume is the case.

24 IT'S NOT JUST THE DEVIL THAT'S IN THE DETAILS

'Human knowledge,' Smiles proposes, *'is but an accumulation of small facts, made by successive generations of men, the little bits of knowledge and experience carefully treasured up by them growing at length into a mighty pyramid.'* Even the smallest stones contribute to that edifice.

'Though many of these facts and observations seemed in the first instance to have but slight significance, they are all found to have their eventual uses, and to fit into their proper places. Even many speculations seemingly remote, turn out to be the basis of results the most practical.'

DEFINING IDEA...

The successful leader must be the master of all details connected with his position.

~ NAPOLEON HILL, AUTHOR OF THINK AND GROW RICH

Smiles goes on to back this up with examples of inventors who took their inspiration from the minute detail of unexpected sources. Sir Samuel Brown, who was studying bridges with a view to building one across the Tweed river, was much taken by a spider's web he saw in the dewy grass and from it took the idea of a structure supported by a web of ropes and chains instead of stones and arches – the suspension bridge. James Watt, the engineer, probably caused some amusement amongst his fellow diners when he seized the jointed carapace of a lobster and studied it. This gave him the inspiration for a jointed iron tube that solved his problem of carrying water under the River Clyde. Finally, Sir Isambard Brunel studied the burrows made by the shipworm to help with the design of the Thames Tunnel.

All of these examples are from the world of physical engineering, but detailed observation of minutiae applies just as much to human social structures, with the added bonus that people are often able to explain their likes, dislikes, and behaviour better than shipworms or boiled lobsters. *'It is the close observation of little things which is the secret of success in business, in art, in science, and in every pursuit in life'*, underlines Smiles.

The converse is also true. Any business that creates an atmosphere in which detail is seen as too petty for the attention of managers is sleepwalking towards a 'no rules' culture with all the inherent dangers that entails. By the time Enron crashed and burned, the senior managers had gone from blasé to blind in their attention to detail. Likewise, rogue trader Nick Leeson of Barings Bank should have been spotted and reined in long before he brought the bank down but senior staff were so happy focusing on what they thought were profits that they ignored or failed to scrutinise the details of the transactions he was engaged in.

HERE'S AN IDEA FOR YOU...

Systematic time and motion studies increase productivity by studying the number of motions used to perform a task. Originally used to study jobs like bricklaying they are just as applicable to anything where people move as they work. A little close observation of your company could end with hours of savings – just by moving the coffee machine, for example.

25 TAKE NOTES

As Smiles observes, *'The practice of writing down thoughts and facts for the purpose of holding them fast and preventing their escape into the dim region of forgetfulness, has been much resorted to by thoughtful and studious men.'*

DEFINING IDEA...

It resembles a tradesman taking stock, without which he never knows either what he possesses or in what he is deficient.

~ JOHN HUNTER, FATHER OF SCIENTIFIC SURGERY, ON TAKING NOTES

Smiles gives many examples of studious note-scribblers who took down anything of importance immediately rather than trusting it to memory. For example, he cites Lord Bacon, who *'left behind him many manuscripts entitled "Sudden thoughts set down for use".'* Note-taking fits in naturally with Smiles' emphasis on detailed observation and constant interpretation. His point is that if we don't carry the means to write down those sudden sparks of brilliance or unexpected observations then we are trusting ourselves to remember them. The problem is that, with the exception of scientists or trainspotters, few of us make sure we always have a notepad to hand.

Taking notes with a pad is not always the best way. It can seem slightly sinister when speaking to people, since it's normally the preserve of journalists or policemen, and both are particularly unsettling. For noting down feedback from workers or customers you may find sound recording is the most discreet option, particularly now that bulky tape recorders have given way to compact digital recorders. If you're going to record a feedback session, however, make sure you don't shove a microphone into the face of your subject. Try not to have it between you and be aware that you will need to chat normally for a few minutes before people relax about the recording enough to speak naturally. If you can touch-type then have a keyboard at hand and slightly to one side (don't have the screen directly between you and your subject) so you can maintain eye contact while typing the notes.

Notes on subjects other than direct speech are probably best written down or typed for easy reference. When it comes to taking notes from texts, Smiles seems much impressed by note-taking extremism: *'Eldon copied Coke upon Littleton twice over with his own hand, so that the book became, as it were, part of his own mind.'* That kind of dedication to detail may be overkill but we all throw away a huge amount of learning because we are out of the habit of jotting down details as we go. It may seem nerdy to pull a pad out and jot notes but if you want to learn as you go, and avoid mistakes from forgetting past lessons, it's a habit worth acquiring.

HERE'S AN IDEA FOR YOU...

Try the Cornell note-taking system. Leave a blank margin down the left side of your page. Take notes on the right-hand side as you go then use the left margin for questions and subject headings – keep these to a few words. The results are far more structured than standard notes.

26 USING THE TOOLS AT HAND

'*The most ordinary occasions will furnish a man with opportunities or suggestions for improvement,*' says Smiles, before adding the crucial proviso, '*if he be but prompt to take advantage of them.*'

DEFINING IDEA...

One needs only to know the twenty-four letters of the alphabet [Greek] in order to learn everything else that one wishes.

~ EDMUND STONE, MATHEMATICIAN

Some years ago, a major US computer publisher was launched in Europe, with offices in a number of different countries. With the launch of the flagship magazine only a few weeks away, I visited two of the offices and found two starkly different scenes. In the first, the staff were at a standstill. It looked like a student sit-in. Asking why, a member of the production team said they didn't have the tool needed to ensure the right workflow so work had ground to a halt.

In the next office, the scene was a frenzy of activity as they finalised the pages. It turned out that they also lacked the tool in question, but they had simply adapted some existing network tools to create a makeshift system. There was one other little difference that made itself noticed: no chairs had been delivered for the staff in the second office but nobody had mentioned that. Instead they had got on with the job of working while standing up. There are cases where a specific tool is essential to a job, but there are many more where work can continue if there is the right sense of urgency and a will to win.

There is also a strong temptation to see the missing tool as an obstacle that cannot be bypassed. Smiles, though, cites the examples of artists without materials who chalked on walls to practise, or Benjamin West who *made his first brushes out of the cat's tail'*. The mathematician Gifford worked out his equations on scraps of leather while working as a cobbler, and the astronomer Rittenhouse first calculated eclipses on his plough handle.

Smiles seems to have neatly rolled two old adages into one — firstly, that it's a poor workman who blames his tools, and secondly that you must strike while the iron is hot (even if it's not the iron you would ideally have chosen). The ballpoint pen was popularised during World War II when the Royal Air Force issued crews with László Bíró's invention in response to the problem that fountain pens stopped working at altitude. It was a great step forward and a brilliant invention. However, while waiting for it to arrive, the aviators had still been making notes while airborne — it was just that they did so using pencils.

HERE'S AN IDEA FOR YOU...

Is a missing tool (be that software, a machine, or staff) stopping you or your staff from progressing? Break the task into its components and see which could be done or at least prepared with what you have in hand. It might be slower or harder but get going with what you've got, not what you want, and you will maintain the momentum.

27 MAKE THE MOST OF EVERY MOMENT

'An hour in every day withdrawn from frivolous pursuits would, if profitably employed, enable a person of ordinary capacity to go far towards mastering a science.' Smiles mainly imagined giving up leisure; today you can glean nearly as much time by re-animating the daily 'dead time.'

DEFINING IDEA...

Work expands so as to fill the time available for its completion. General recognition of this fact is shown in the proverbial phrase, 'It is the busiest man who has time to spare.'

– C. NORTHCOTE PARKINSON, WRITER

Smiles reels off a long list of the great and good who used moments of downtime to learn something else: *'Dr Mason Good translated Lucretius while riding in his carriage in the streets of London, going the round of his patients. Dr Darwin composed nearly all his works in the same way while driving about in his "sulky" [a type of carriage] from house to house in the country, writing down his thoughts on little scraps of paper, which he carried about with him for the purpose.'*

His list also incudes the writer Kirke White who learnt Greek while walking to and from the office, and Daguesseau, Chancellor of France, who wrote an entire book *'in the successive intervals of waiting for dinner'*. Elihu Burritt, the blacksmith turned mathematician, *'attributed his first success in self-improvement, not to genius, which he disclaimed, but simply to the careful employment of those invaluable fragments of time called "odd moments".'* Today's odd moments add up to more than you think. The many minutes we spend in queues, waiting outside an office to see someone, on the bus hoping the lift will arrive soon, or just hanging around, soon add up, meaning that every full day involves a surprising amount of 'dead time.' The free newspapers commonly given out to commuters are hard evidence that with a little creativity it is possible to build an entire industry out of the daily 'dead time' of others. An Ipsos Reid study for Research In Motion (the makers of the BlackBerry) suggests that a typical working day includes at least 60 minutes of unused time that can be clawed back if we use it productively. Clearly Research In Motion tends to interpret 'productively' as 'emailing with a BlackBerry' but 60 minutes a day means 250 hours of your life every year in which to learn a language, master a skill, or advance your knowledge – providing, of course, that you have the means to do so at hand.

If Kirke White was able to learn Greek while walking then it's not unreasonable for any of us to try to learn French, Spanish, or astrophysics in the traffic jams on the way to work, and there are plenty of tapes and CDs available to help you do it.

HERE'S AN IDEA FOR YOU...

iPods and MP3 players aren't just for music. Sign up to a podcast service and you'll find lectures, briefings, and language lessons that you can download to your player or phone, which you can slip it into your pocket ready to listen to on the train, in the car, or just while waiting for the bill.

28 ALL OR NOTHING

'Never stop till the thing is done,' was the watchword of John Hunter, the master surgeon who Smiles singles out for his approach to projects.

Hunter's maxim is really two parts. The second part is never to stop once you've started out. But importantly, the first part of his maxim is only to start out once you're completely sure that the job in hand is worthwhile and doable: *"My rule is, deliberately to consider, before I commence, whether the thing be practicable. If it be not practicable, I do not attempt it."*

The importance of this is often overlooked. How many times have we all blundered into an undertaking out of a vague sense of duty, or nagging, or peer pressure only to realise part way through that it is not within our scope, talents, or time? Part of Hunter's genius was that he coldly considered whether he could get to the end of any journey he set out on and if he didn't think he could do so then he refused to start out. It's an approach that is entirely compatible with the concept of visualisation since it means picturing the end game of a project before starting out and being entirely comfortable with that and with the steps that will be required to get to it.

The second part was the commitment he brought to tasks having accepted that, yes, he could finish the job: *"If it be practicable, I can accomplish it if I give sufficient pains to it; and having begun, I never stop till the thing is done. To this rule I owe all my success."* Which is a more elegant statement of the old adage that *'winners never quit, and quitters never win'.*

Take that just a little further and you have one of the key maxims of Napoleon Hill, author of *Think and Grow Rich*, who believed that: *"Every person who wins in any undertaking must be willing to burn his ships and cut all sources of retreat. Only by so doing can one be sure of maintaining that state of mind known as a burning desire to win, essential to success."*

Hill's maxim is more strongly worded, but it is a reasonable extension of Hunter's – if you enter into an undertaking, you should do so confident that you will soldier to the finish with no turning back. In effect it's a question of determination and, in particular, of examining your motivation, chances of success and degree of commitment before embarking on a project rather than halfway in when initial enthusiasm is waning and the full extent of the difficulty is becoming apparent.

HERE'S AN IDEA FOR YOU...

Not sure about taking on a project? Imagine that there is simply no escape route or exit strategy; that not completing the project would be total failure leading to the loss of your job or business. If you are still confident, then it's time to put foot to floor. If you hesitate, then maybe, like Hunter, you should walk away.

29 WINNING OVER RESISTANCE

Jenner invented vaccination, using cowpox to render people immune to the fatal smallpox. How was that received? *'First with indifference, then with active hostility.'* To impose your policies you are going to have to win over resistance.

DEFINING IDEA...

Don't think, but try; be patient, be accurate.

~ JOHN HUNTER'S ADVICE ON INTRODUCING CONTROVERSIAL CHANGE

Jenner's discovery of vaccination is a classic Smiles example of both genius and perseverance. Jenner had heard repeatedly that milkmaids working with cow herds infected with cowpox did not then suffer from smallpox. At a time when the medical world dismissed this evidence out of hand, he came to the conclusion that the one appeared to work as a preventative of the other. With careful methodology he investigated the approach of deliberately infecting people with cowpox to stave off smallpox. In the process, however, because he was transferring tissue from an animal to a person, Jenner's lifesaving discovery managed to upset both the medical world and the church.

'Vaccination was denounced from the pulpit as "diabolical". It was averred that vaccinated children became "ox-faced", that abscesses broke out to "indicate sprouting horns", and that the countenance was gradually "transmuted into the visage of a cow, the voice into the bellowing of bulls".' Quite what Jenner thought of this wild-eyed paranoia in denunciation of his methodically researched and carefully implemented scientific discovery is something we can only wonder at. Given the degree of hysteria he ran into, he must have

feared that his breakthrough would founder on unreasoning resistance. The medical profession wasn't quite so colourful in its resistance but it did simmer with the resentment reserved for any groundbreaking newcomer in any field of human endeavour. The first people who allowed themselves to be vaccinated were pelted with stones and forced to hide indoors, such was the paranoia and panic generated by the practice.

Fortunately, Jenner had studied under John Hunter, another great favourite of Smiles, who had told him the best defence was to be right. Jenner certainly practised what he preached since he vaccinated his own son as part of his research. In the end, Jenner's second breakthrough (the first being the discovery) came with the help of Lady Ducie and the Countess of Berkeley, who Jenner convinced sufficiently that they had their own children vaccinated. Clearly, celebrity endorsement was as effective then as it is now and at long last Jenner found fame and reward.

There are several lessons here: firstly, don't expect to be welcomed with open arms because you happen to be delivering a lifesaver; secondly, stick with your beliefs despite ridicule and hostility; and, thirdly, aim to broaden your support base if you want to have your methods accepted.

HERE'S AN IDEA FOR YOU...

The importance of Lady Ducie and the Countess of Berkeley can't be underplayed as Jenner brought influential people in as stakeholders in an enterprise. If you are introducing change, look for similarly influential figures and convert them first. Then use them as advocates to convince others, rather than fighting by yourself.

30 LOOK AND LEARN

Richard Foley, a nailmaker from Stourbridge heard that Swedish nail factories had hit on a much cheaper means of manufacture. So he disappeared. *'No one knew whither he had gone, not even his own family, for he had not informed them of his intention, lest he should fail.'* He had gone abroad to learn at source.

DEFINING IDEA...

All of the top achievers I know are life-long learners... looking for new skills, insights, and ideas. If they're not learning, they're not growing... not moving toward excellence.

– DENIS WAITLEY, MOTIVATIONAL SPEAKER AND AUTHOR OF THE SEEDS OF GREATNESS

In the 1950s and 60s, the Japanese travelled widely looking at American and European manufacturing. Within a few years they were imitating it, then surpassing it. In some cases, the original industries they had copied declined almost to the point of disappearance – the British motorbike industry, for example, went from a position of world domination to near extinction. In the mid 1980s, one man, John Bloor, returned the favour by going to Japan and studying just what it was that made Japanese motorbike manufacture so successful. He learnt his lesson well and returned to the UK to revive the Triumph motorbike brand, which is now once more running with the pack leaders.

Smiles observed exactly the same approach in that Stourbridge nailmaker, although Foley took the idea to an extreme that would probably be judged as industrial espionage today. Foley had taken his fiddle and worked his passage to Sweden before begging and busking his way to the Dannemora mines near Upsala. It seems life for nail workers and miners was just as dull as we imagine and the iron men were delighted to have a distraction from making and splitting iron, which, as it turned out, was the technique that they had mastered and which had given them the competitive edge.

Foley returned and tried to recreate the iron-splitting machines he had seen, only to meet with failure as his new-found technical knowledge proved incomplete. So he picked up his fiddle again and returned to his Swedish friends. It seems he appeared such a simple and open soul that he was again welcomed into the heart of the business and this time he made extensive drawings of those parts of the machines that had not worked in his own copies. Returning home a second time he tried again and this time found himself the sole manufacturer in England in possession of the technology. Fame and fortune followed.

For Smiles this is a particularly revealing story since it shows not only the imagination to literally go further than his fellows but also the perseverance to keep on trying after initial failure. Playing the fiddle might be an optional extra, but the lesson is clear that it pays to travel, study the opposition and make use of what you learn.

HERE'S AN IDEA FOR YOU...

Arrange a study tour. You don't have to stoop to industrial espionage – just don't apply to direct rivals and expect them to open their doors to you. Apply to equivalent companies in different business sectors or different regions and offer an exchange trip to learn from each other. Just make sure you learn more from them than they do from you.

31 VISUALISING VICTORY

'It is related of a young French officer, that he used to walk about his apartment exclaiming, "I will be Marshal of France and a great general." His ardent desire was the presentiment of his success; for the young officer did become a distinguished commander, and he died a Marshal of France.'

DEFINING IDEA...

Learn to think like a winner. Think positive and visualise your strengths.

~ VIC BRADEN, TENNIS COACH

It's not the idea of a mantra that Smiles is advocating here, but willpower and, in particular, the force of visualisation – of getting our minds into the habit of envisaging our own success as an essential step towards achieving it. Want it enough, picture it clearly enough, and you are part-way there already: *'An intense anticipation itself transforms possibility into reality; our desires being often but the precursors of the things which we are capable of performing.'* There's a flipside to this coin. If you continue to see yourself as mediocre or ordinary, then the chances are you will stay that way. *'The timid and hesitating find everything impossible, chiefly because it seems so.'*

The power of visualisation is remarkable. It is now a common practice among sports coaches to instruct athletes to visualise their own success because not only does this help make them winners psychologically but there is also evidence to suggest it improves physical performance, with the body taking on board intense visualisation as if it were experience itself. Unfortunately, the negative power of visualisation is just as forceful. It's often said that the difference between winners and losers is that the former visualise their success while the latter dwell on the implications of failure. By thinking yourself into that negative mindset you become demotivated and reduce your own chances of success.

In terms of self-help, the lesson is very clear – see yourself as you want to be. If you don't, nobody else will, and it is certainly true that if you see something as too difficult to try then you are undoubtedly doomed to fail.

Visualisation and mantras are not to be confused. Just muttering to yourself that 'every day, in every way, I'm getting better and better' is about as likely to bring about a change in your life as asking the mirror who's the most beautiful of them all. The Marshal of France didn't get to where he wanted by saying it; he got there because his goal was achievable, he desired it passionately, and stating that out loud was a daily reminder to himself to keep faith with the pact he had made with his own ambition. Enter into a similar pact with yourself: picture it, believe it, and you will get there – though experience suggests it very often takes a little longer than you'd like.

HERE'S AN IDEA FOR YOU...

Employ Napoleon Hill's six steps: 1) Decide exactly what you want; 2) Decide what you are prepared to give; 3) Fix a deadline for your goal; 4) Create the plan to get there and start now – ready or not; 5) Write out your game plan, with goals, costs and deadline; 6) Read that game plan aloud daily as you get up, and as you go to bed. As you read it, picture it.

32 GO FOR THE THROAT

'It is rapid decision, and a promptitude in action, such as taking instant advantage of an enemy's mistakes, that so often wins battles,' notes Smiles, and uses Napoleon as his example. In business, nothing whatsoever has changed since then.

DEFINING IDEA...

Two armies are two bodies which meet and endeavour to frighten each other: a moment of panic occurs, and that moment must be turned to advantage.

~ NAPOLEON BONAPARTE

At Arcola, Napoleon claims to have won the battle with only twenty-five horsemen. Smiles quotes the Corsican as saying: *'I seized a moment of lassitude, gave every man a trumpet, and gained the day with this handful.'* It seems ludicrous that a couple of dozen troops could change the shape of an entire battle, but really, as Napoleon notes, it is not their strength that is the question, but rather the perfect moment to take advantage of the others' weakness. Similarly, Sun Tzu declares that *"if the enemy leaves a door open, you must rush in"*. In business, as in battle, the time to pounce is that moment of weakness when your opponents leave their throats exposed.

In the early 1990s, Ashton Tate and Borland were giants of the software industry. This was a time when entire companies grew up around single products – WordStar and WordPerfect battled each other with their rival word processors and each had a loyal following; Lotus lived off the proceeds from a single spreadsheet. Ashton Tate and Borland each believed the other to be their only rival. Remarkably, they appeared to spend entire development budgets on adding new features to their databases rather than worry about diversification. Then Ashton Tate produced dBASE IV, the fourth major version of its software and the critical reaction was very negative. So many bugs and instabilities were found that users either held off from upgrading from earlier versions or decided to wait for the next version before making the move. Borland believed it had a chance to step in and wipe its competitor off the map by buying Ashton Tate in 1991 and looked set to dominate the database market from that point on.

Nowadays, you probably haven't even heard of Borland or Ashton Tate, nor for that matter WordPerfect or WordStar. You probably can't even imagine going out and buying (or downloading) a stand-alone word processing package because you almost certainly use one that came with an entire suite of other common office utilities. That's because while the industry giants squared up head to head, tearing chunks out of each other and waiting for their rival to fall, a smarter, more agile company called Microsoft was busy spreading the idea of the office suite in which spreadsheets, databases, and word processors were all bundled together and released as one. Like mammals watching the dinosaurs roar, the next generation of competition was watching for the weak spot and waiting for its moment. Borland thought Ashton Tate's moment of weakness was its chance – in reality it signalled the end of dominance for a generation of companies.

HERE'S AN IDEA FOR YOU...

You should have contingency plans for disasters in your own line of work – strikes, fire, etc. – but do you have contingency plans for your rivals' disasters? Draw up a plan of action to put in place should your competitors fall flat on their face tomorrow.

33 LEAD FROM THE FRONT

Quoting from General Napier, Smiles says: *'The great art of commanding is to take a fair share of the work.'* Leading from the front involves inspiring the troops by doing, as much as by saying.

Smiles believed that great leaders spend more time walking the walk than talking the talk. In Napier's case, he tells the tale of the battle of Meeanee in India – *'one of the most extraordinary feats in history'*. With just 2,000 men, of which only 400 were trained European troops, Napier took on a force of 35,000 Beloochees, charging their ranks and driving them back through sheer belligerence. *'It is this sort of pluck, tenacity, and determined perseverance which wins soldiers' battles, and, indeed, every battle,'* concludes Smiles.

DEFINING IDEA...

If you want something said, ask a man. If you want something done, ask a woman.

– MARGARET THATCHER

Much as Napoleon believed there was a perfect moment to strike, Smiles asserts that it is more likely to present itself to the fighter who presses home an attack and goes the extra mile: *'Though your force be less than another's, you equal and outmaster your opponent if you continue it longer and concentrate it more.'* For Smiles, the role of leadership is to provide the inspiration for that final push, and Napier's ethos perfectly fitted this line of thinking. *"The man who leads an army,"* according to Napier, *"cannot succeed unless his whole mind is thrown into his work. The more trouble, the more labour must be given; the more danger, the more pluck must be shown, till all is overpowered."*

Many of the most famous businessmen are those who have inspired a company and moulded it around their own ethos. At Microsoft, Bill Gates was renowned for his 'bandwidth' in being able to engage with problems big or small concerning any aspect of the business. Richard Branson's energetic, try-harder lifestyle is the key weapon of his multinational brand. Stelios Haji-Ioannou of EasyJet is renowned for working the aisles of aircraft and apologising to angry passengers in person. Whether or not Steve Jobs is truly up to speed with all of the workings of the latest iPhone, he is revered within his company as a man with an engineer's mind and a designer's eye. When Jobs returned to Apple after leaving for a while to run Next, the company's fortunes almost immediately turned around.

Consider the stark contrast between these leaders and the approach of Gerald Ratner when he had his 'Ratner' moment and declared his company's products to be "total crap". Whatever it was that possessed him to ridicule his own jewellery business certainly provided him with an instant lesson in how to lose the support of your army.

HERE'S AN IDEA FOR YOU...

The business equivalent of leading your force into the heart of an enraged enemy is to personally face up to angry clients instead of leaving it to others. Make a point of asking where there is customer dissatisfaction and be seen to meet it head on and in person.

34 THINK AHEAD

One classic business mistake is failing to plan for success. A growing venture will demand more staff, and more training. Follow the example of Jonas Hanway who, Smiles tells us, responded to the rumour of a French invasion by turning *'his attention to the best mode of keeping up the supply of seamen'.*

DEFINING IDEA...

I always say we don't have a worker shortage in this country, we have a skill shortage... This is an economy that needs skilled workers and what we're trying to do is manage the change that is taking place and help provide those skills so that more positions can be filled.

~ ALEXIS HERMAN, US SECRETARY OF LABOUR

Jonas Hanway *'summoned a meeting of merchants and shipowners at the Royal Exchange, and there proposed to them to form themselves into a society for fitting out landsmen volunteers and boys, to serve on board the king's ships.'* To fully understand the importance of Jonas's actions we should remember that this was a time in which the standard response to a shortage of seamen was to club drunks over the head on their way home, or turn out anyone from the prisons who had a full complement of limbs.

Modern businesses aren't usually quite that desperate when it comes to recruiting but a surprising number of them embark on projects with the vague (and often undiscussed) policy that they will recruit skilled workers as and when they need them. That's just fine, unless that skill turns out to be in demand in which case you are suddenly competing with every other employer and consequently bidding against them in a seller's market. Regardless of whether or not the year 2000 bug was the threat it was believed to be, it certainly exposed the danger of failing to plan for skills shortages. Computer programmers became so much in demand that companies found themselves competing with each other to retain their services. Many found themselves having to make do with insufficient staff – some even ended up paying just for the option to access IT workers' time.

What Jonas did in response to the need for seamen was establish The Marine Society, 'an institution which has proved of much national advantage, and it is to this day of great and substantial utility'. Although the rumours of French invasion have died down a little these days, the Marine Society still exists.

Truly successful sports clubs establish 'academies' for the would-be stars of the future. One factor in David Beckham's successful relationship with Manchester United was a loyalty kindled when he trained with the club as an aspiring junior. That's precisely the kind of long-termism you want to encourage when it comes to skilled workers for a company, particularly if the company operates in one of the more cutting-edge arenas such as knowledge working or financial services.

HERE'S AN IDEA FOR YOU...

If your resources won't stretch to a full-blown academy, or indeed any internal training at all, then look to a third party, but don't just accept a menu of off-the-shelf skills courses if your own activities are breaking new ground. Find a training company that will agree to work with you to help forge your next generation of front-line fighters.

35 THE POWER OF ONE

'The life of Granville Sharp,' Smiles tells us, *'is another striking example of the power of ... individual energy – a power which was afterwards transfused into the noble band of workers in the cause of Slavery Abolition.'* Sometimes it only takes one person to stand up against the status quo and change it.

DEFINING IDEA...

The power of one, if fearless and focused, is formidable, but the power of many working together is better.
~ GLORIA MACAPAGAL-ARROYO, FILIPINA POLITICIAN

Whilst a number of men, including Clarkson, Wilberforce, Buxton and Brougham, were instrumental in the abolition of slavery, Smiles singles out Sharp as *'the first, and perhaps the greatest of them all, in point of perseverance, energy, and intrepidity'*. Sharp's fate was changed by a meeting with a slave, Jonathan Strong, cast out by his master as being of no further use, and now begging and gravely ill. Sharp got Strong admitted to hospital and eventually found him a job but some years later his original owner recognised him and demanded him back. Strong appealed to Sharp and Sharp decided not to let the man be enslaved again, thereby starting off a protracted legal process about the nature of personal liberty.

At this time, the law about personal liberty was vague and confusing. Initially Sharp faced a deluge of legal opinion telling him the law was against him and that Strong's previous owner still had a claim on the man. Sharp, however, refused to back down and instead dug tirelessly through laws until he established that *'there is nothing in any English law or statute – at least that I am able to find out – that can justify the enslaving of others'*. In other words he stepped away from the problem as being one of disputed property and looked instead for a legal basis for slavery itself.

Sharp wrote a hugely influential tract decrying the whole trade and questioning its legality and in doing so exposed its vileness and aroused public opinion against it. In test cases he managed to establish that no man could be a slave in England, thereby paving the way for the abolition of the entire trade. Since Britain effectively ruled the seas at that point in time, Sharp could be credited with setting in motion a process that was to have truly global significance.

What Sharp proved was that it only takes decent people doing nothing for bad practice to take hold. By bringing slavery to the forefront of people's attention and questioning whether it should be allowed to happen, he managed to create sufficient strength of feeling to have that evil made illegal. Accept substandard practices and not only do you damn yourself to them but you (and your company) are setting yourself up to be leapfrogged by the next rival with the motivation to do something about it.

HERE'S AN IDEA FOR YOU...

Is there an aspect of your business practice that you have questioned only to meet with shrugs of 'what can you do'? Don't ask everyone concerned whether they think it can be changed. Instead ask whether they personally agree with it. Demonstrate that a majority of stakeholders dislike something and you are already on the way to making it better.

36 BIG BUSINESS AND BIG BUSINESSMEN

Never think there's something mean about doing business, unless you are yourself a mean person. As Smiles says: *'It has been a favourite fallacy with dunces in all times, that men of genius are unfitted for business, as well as that business occupations unfit men for the pursuits of genius.'*

DEFINING IDEA...

Seest thou a man diligent in his business? He shall stand before kings.

~ PROVERBS OF SOLOMON

We still talk about business as if it were a dirty process. We 'roll up our sleeves' and 'get our hands dirty' in the pursuit of 'dirty cash' and 'filthy lucre' but there is nothing inherently demeaning about business itself. Smiles tells us: *'All work that brings honest gain is honourable, whether it be of hand or mind. The fingers may be soiled, yet the heart remains pure; for it is not material so much as moral dirt that defiles – greed far more than grime, and vice than verdigris.'*

He goes on to list great men who have combined their achievements with work – Plato who traded in oil, Spinoza who polished glass, Linnaeus who made shoes. Chaucer was a soldier, Milton a schoolmaster, and Newton certainly must have rubbed up against a lot of filthy lucre when he worked in the Royal Mint.

Smiles would have had little time for all those people who apologise for their jobs when asked what they do, and even less for any who blame their job for the ordinariness of their existence. His approach would be to make the most of what presented itself by working ever harder at the job in hand. Too many people fall into the trap of doing a job desultorily and blaming that job for their blues. In fact, doing a job half-heartedly is a self-destructive approach, likely to do you no favours. Firstly, you are sapping your own self-esteem by telling yourself you don't want to do something you keep doing, then by not throwing yourself into it you are limiting your experimentation in life, and because you will strike others as being uncommitted you damage your reputation. That's not even considering the effect on the job.

The answer is to give it your all and only then, if you can honestly say you've done that, can you see the job as being beneath you, in which case it's your own responsibility to move on. Or, as James L. Hayes, former president of the American Management Association put it: *"When a mature and able manager feels bored, he should seriously consider changing jobs, changing companies or simply retiring. It is not fair to anyone for half a leader to hold a full-time leadership job."*

HERE'S AN IDEA FOR YOU...

Bored? Frustrated? Go the extra mile. Draw up five ways in which you can go above and beyond what is expected of you in your role. Now put the plan into action. You can't truly claim to have exhausted the possibilities of a job until you have stretched its boundaries.

37 YOU MAKE YOUR OWN LUCK

Smiles' conviction that the power to improve lies entirely in our own hands means that he was not a believer in the idea of bad luck: *'It will often be found that men who are constantly lamenting their luck, are in some way or other reaping the consequences of their own neglect, mismanagement, improvidence, or want of application.'*

Smiles' view is that bad luck is often nothing more than a cover for personal underperformance. By the same token if you want a little more good luck in your life then it's time to go out and make some.

DEFINING IDEA...

All of us have bad luck and good luck. The man who persists through the bad luck – who keeps right on going – is the man who is there when the good luck comes, and is ready to receive it.
– ROBERT COLLIER,
AMERICAN MOTIVATIONAL AUTHOR

Psychologist Richard Wiseman conducted thousands of interviews of 'lucky' and 'unlucky' people to try to find a pattern. What he found was that attitude is the key, with those who see themselves as lucky often turning out to be people with a will to turn bad luck to good and make the best of a bad job. He also found that 'lucky' people are simply those who are open to possibility – they see opportunities that are there for everyone but which other people aren't aware of enough to see or grasp.

Wiseman draws a major distinction between chance and luck. His point is that chance events, like winning the lottery are things we have no control over and don't consistently happen to the same person. He says that chance events have less impact than we like to think: *"You might say, 'Fifty percent of my life is due to chance events.' No, it isn't. Maybe 10% is. That other 40% that you think you're having no influence over is actually defined by the way you think."*

The trick is to be open to new experiences. Another of Wiseman's findings was that 'unlucky' people are stuck in routines. *"When they see something new, they want no part of it. Lucky people always want something new. They're prepared to take risks and relaxed enough to see the opportunities in the first place."*

Tempting though it is to bemoan bad luck, it's all too often an excuse for poor application, or an inability to see the good side of developments. Smiles says: *'We have heard of a person of this sort, who went so far as to declare his belief that if he had been a hatter, people would have been born without heads! There is however a Russian proverb which says that Misfortune is next door to Stupidity.'* Believers in bad luck would do well to open their eyes.

HERE'S AN IDEA FOR YOU...

Take up Wiseman's four principles to get lucky: 1) maximize opportunities – keep your eyes open for opportunity; 2) listen to your luck – trust your intuition and gut feelings; 3) expect good fortune – believe the future is bright and it will be; 4) turn bad luck into good – look for the silver lining.

38 ONE THING AT A TIME

The secret to getting a lot of things done, says Smiles, is not to try to do them all at once. Instead he quotes the preacher Reverend Richard Cecil whose motto was *'the shortest way to do many things is to do only one thing at once'*

DEFINING IDEA...

I never could have done what I have done without the habits of punctuality, order, and diligence, without the determination to concentrate myself on one subject at a time.

~ CHARLES DICKENS

'Method is essential,' instructs Smiles, *'and enables a larger amount of work to be got through with satisfaction'.* Reverend Cecil likens method to packing things in a box: *"A good packer will get in half as much again as a bad one.'* Smiles also cites the Dutch politician Jan de Witt, saying: *"If I have any necessary despatches to make, I think of nothing else till they are finished; if domestic affairs require my attention, I give myself wholly up to them till they are set in order."*

In these days of information overload we often find a whole number of different tasks demanding our attention or distracting us from the principle project. Human nature being what it is, we can easily allow such distractions to keep us from work because we are most likely to put off the things we don't like in favour of those that are more pleasant. Getting on with the job becomes ever harder as emails, text messages, phone calls, and instant messaging all break into our time, shatter our concentration, and distract us. Reverend Cecil's answer seems to apply even more in these days of multiple communication channels, as anyone who's ever tried to enjoy lunch with a BlackBerry user will attest. That's not to say that communication technologies are bad, but we often show poor discipline, not to mention pure bad manners when it comes to using them. Nicolas Sarkozy, the President of France caused outrage in his (largely Catholic) country when he was seen on TV checking his mobile phone for messages in the middle of an audience with the Pope. If ever there was an example of bad 'packing', that was it.

Instead of trying to do everything at once, try a little personal project management and break tasks down into categories of 'urgent', 'important', 'good to get done', and 'non-essential'. If you can delegate any of those tasks, do so. Likewise, if you can eliminate any of the non-essentials, do that too. Now set to work on the urgent stuff and don't allow anything else to get in the way. Ideally if you do this regularly then fewer things will reach the urgent stage because your time management means you will have tackled them before they reach that point. Set precise times for when you will allow yourself to get up and have coffee breaks or go for lunch and be firm with yourself about what time you intend to finish work because without that deadline you will be less productive and the job will creep on into the night.

HERE'S AN IDEA FOR YOU...

Do you respond to emails throughout the day? Try instead setting aside a time slot morning and evening and only dealing with email at those times. Let your clients and colleagues know that's what you do and you'll find they don't see you as any less responsive and will often start to send fewer distracting emails.

39 KEEP FIT

'Practical success in life depends more upon physical health than is generally imagined,' Smiles tells us – centuries before governments hit on recommendations of exercise.

'Work educates the body, as study educates the mind,' Smiles declares, showing a fine understanding of what we now understand to be the principles of physical training. *'It is said that the Duke of Wellington, when once looking on at the boys engaged in their sports in the play-ground at Eton, where he had spent many of his own younger days, made the remark, "It was there that the battle of Waterloo was won!"'* Smiles' implication is not simply that physical fitness has a part to play in the physical nature of soldiering, but that it inspired Wellington to a more successful attitude.

By contrast, he suggests that a lack of fitness and activity leaves people more inclined to depression: *'It is perhaps to the neglect of physical exercise that we find amongst students so frequent a tendency towards discontent, unhappiness, inaction, and reverie.'* As then, so it is now, with a growing body of studies showing us that physical fitness is an invaluable weapon in the boardroom, not least because it helps counter stress. A sensible fitness regime helps keep that waistline at bay, which goes a long way towards easing self-esteem issues and can improve confidence. It also boosts lung and heart capacity, which combat the known physical ill-effects of stress, including tension, high blood pressure and low resistance to sickness. By encouraging better sleep it can also help deal with anxiety and the pressures of the working day, quite possibly making us more productive in the process. Quite simply, it can make us feel like winners and as we've seen elsewhere in Smiles' *Self-help*, feeling like a winner is halfway to being one.

Don't worry: there's no need to leap onto gym machines or squeeze yourself into lycra like some kind of spandex saveloy. Fitness can come simply from increasing your activity levels and that could be shopping, golf, walking the dog or cycling to work. Indeed you're more likely to keep up a fitness regime if it's an integral part of your daily life, like going to work, than you are if it is an alien process like going to the gym. And don't think that the amount you spent on membership is going to get you into the gym – that doesn't work, and gyms all over the world owe their survival to the vast numbers of new members who pay up in January and are never seen again after February.

HERE'S AN IDEA FOR YOU...

Build up your exercise gradually. Use a folding bike to get to the train station. Get off your bus a stop early and walk the rest of the way. Take the stairs rather than the lift. If you succeed in making these little changes to your daily routine it will probably last longer than any promise of gym-going and end up saving you money and shedding those pounds.

40 PRACTICE MAKES PERFECT

'Everything that we learn is the mastery of a difficulty; and the mastery of one helps to the mastery of others,' says Smiles. *'The danseuse who turns a pirouette, the violinist who plays a sonata, have acquired their dexterity by patient repetition and after many failures.'*

DEFINING IDEA...

If I am to speak for ten minutes, I need a week for preparation; if fifteen minutes, three days; if half an hour, two days; if an hour, I am ready now.
~ WOODROW T. WILSON

Curiously, even though we all know that practice makes perfect, we try to avoid practising anything as adults apart from, perhaps, a golf swing. We seem averse to dress rehearsals and run-throughs when it comes to business events, forever hoping to wing it on the day. The price we pay for this is usually to live in dread of big meetings and presentations rather than to face up to them and rehearse. This is flawed thinking at best. Not only do we do ourselves no favours by leaving our performance up to chance on the day but also we suffer more by hiding from the fear than we would by staring it down in a series of practice runs.

Smiles gives the example of Jack Curran, orator and lawyer, who was stung by his early failure in debates (he stuttered and was reduced to silence by nerves). He overcame his problems by *reading aloud, emphatically and distinctly, the best passages in literature, for several hours every day, studying his features before a mirror, and adopting a method of gesticulation suited to his rather awkward and ungraceful figure.'*

Talking to yourself has always had a bit of a bad rep as the first sign of madness. This is a shame because I for one have long talked to myself to practise arguments and even argued both sides of a case. I'll admit that arguing with yourself could be considered as borderline barmy but I work on the principle that you've only tipped over the edge if you start losing the arguments. Of course, these days you only have to put on a hands-free headset and you can rant like a madman in public without anyone paying the slightest bit of attention.

So, get into the habit. Practise those presentations, pitches and board meetings by speaking aloud. Then move on to full rehearsals with an audience – preferably a sympathetic one. Ask for feedback and don't be put off if that feedback isn't as positive as you hoped. You may feel silly but it's better to feel silly now and excel on the day than to find yourself on a podium running through your speech notes for the first time with dozens of 'impress me' faces staring at you like lions at feeding time.

HERE'S AN IDEA FOR YOU...

Can't bear to rehearse in front of an audience? Then deliver your presentation or sales pitch to a video camera. Most digital cameras and even phone cameras can handle at least a few minutes these days. Watch the playback to get an idea of how you look and sound.

41 BEING BACKWARDS ABOUT COMING FORWARDS

'A barking dog is often more useful than a sleeping lion,' observes Smiles, implying that modesty can be overrated if it means that you don't let your merits shine or come to the attention of your peers.

Smiles quotes the American author Washington Irving as saying: *"As for the talk about modest merit being neglected, it is too often a cant, by which indolent and irresolute men seek to lay their want of success at the door of the public."* Clearly, Irving suspects here that modesty is nothing more than an excuse for a more deep-seated lack of drive, but he goes on to clarify that even genuine modesty runs the risk of simply going unnoticed.

DEFINING IDEA...

There's one blessing only, the source and cornerstone of beatitude – confidence in self.
– SENECA

Irving also goes on to reject criticism of those who are not backwards about coming forwards since *"there is a lot of cant too about the success of forward and impudent men, while men of retiring worth are passed over with neglect. But it usually happens that those forward men have that valuable quality of promptness and activity without which worth is a mere inoperative property."* Smiles passes no comment on Irving's views, but he presents more of Irving's thoughts than almost all of the hundreds of individuals he holds up as examples so it seems fair to say that he shared the opinion.

This leaves a bit of a quandary for the genuinely talented yet modest. While Irving is right to point out that a lot of 'forward men' are actually those who are prepared to seize the moment and propose themselves for attention, that doesn't mean they are all deeply talented. I'm sure we can all think of someone who has made it to where they are through their talent for self-publicity rather than anything more profound. Nonetheless, Irving is also right that anyone with abilities who keeps quiet about them is of no use to other individuals or an organisation in need of knowing not only who can do what, but also whether they are confident in doing it.

One possible solution is the approach taken by a consultant who does talent audits for digital design companies and advertising agencies. Essentially she interviews their staff and finds out what skills they have. In the world of technology, a lot of programming, scripting, and design skills are largely self-taught and so the companies are usually sitting on a wealth of talent they are unaware of. Of course, you could say that it is down to the individuals to publicise that fact, but they already have roles and often the first that the company knows of their alternative talent is when those individuals take it elsewhere to start another job working with that skill in another company.

HERE'S AN IDEA FOR YOU...

Feel passed over? Have a skill you would like to exploit but currently don't? Draw up a list of the top three skills you have which you feel are unrecognised. Now try to match those skills with a possible mentor — someone in the organisation or same line of work who will understand your skills and encourage them.

42 FIFTEEN MINUTES

Smiles frequently points out the power of small changes, saying that, *'it is the repetition of little acts which constitute not only the sum of human character, but which determine the character of nations'*. For Smiles, it can take as little as fifteen minutes a day to make a difference.

'Fifteen minutes a day devoted to self-improvement will be felt at the end of the year,' Smiles declares, while noting that *'an hour wasted daily in trifles or in indolence, would, if devoted to self-improvement, make an ignorant man wise in a few years, and employed in good works, would make his life fruitful, and death a harvest of worthy deeds'.*

DEFINING IDEA...

If you have never said 'Excuse me' to a parking meter or bashed your shins on a fireplug, you are probably wasting too much valuable reading time.
~ SHERRI CHASIN CALVO, SCIENCE WRITER

Most of us baulk at the idea of setting aside an hour a day for self-improvement, even if we currently spend that long in the pub or sitting in front of computer games. Fifteen minutes, on the other hand, is a whole different ball game. Who honestly can't possibly put aside fifteen minutes to dedicate to learning something?

Fifteen minutes a day spent learning a language is more use than the traditional format of an hourly lesson once a week, not least because you are fresher and it promotes the repetition needed to pick up new phrases. I once worked for a language school that specialised in teaching English to French business people. The key to its success was that as well as face-to-face lessons it insisted on follow-up lessons by phone twice a week. These were fifteen minutes long and encouraged the students to practise their new language in phone conversations (which is where they would mostly be using it) and in bite-sized morsels about relevant subjects. While every student seemed to see the classes as something of a duty, they never failed to make time for the phone calls.

Horace Mann, one of the driving forces behind public education in the US, advocated reading a little every day. Like Smiles, he saw fifteen minutes a day as being enough to make a significant difference over the course of a year. Studies in Japan suggest that fifteen minutes of puzzling your grey cells every day can help keep those synapses firing and may even slow the effects of ageing on the brain.

The point is that it doesn't take a huge investment in time to make huge advances in learning – just as long as you stick with it. The beauty of the fifteen-minute approach is that it's so short it shouldn't become a chore or something that you continually put off because you can't find the time. As such you're more likely to stick with it over the full course of the year than those weekly language classes.

HERE'S AN IDEA FOR YOU...

Looking for fifteen minutes of language learning? Try online language courses, which offer snippets of study to complete at your own pace and for a number of different levels. Googling will give you any number of language courses but try the BBC at www.bbc.co.uk for a helpful (and free) starting point.

43 TIME WASTING

As much as Smiles values the wonders of hard work, he doesn't believe in life being enslaved to business. He champions the importance of leisure time: *'An economical use of time is the true mode of securing leisure: it enables us to get through business and carry it forward instead of being driven by it.'*

DEFINING IDEA...

Half the time men think they are talking business they are wasting time.

~ EDGAR WATSON HOWE, AMERICAN NOVELIST AND ESSAYIST

There's a misleading fallacy that the more time you spend at work the better a worker you are. Long hours in the office, lunch breaks snatched at the keyboard and perpetual answering of emails at any time of night or day do not actually equate to good working practice. It might even mean the opposite, with employees feeling insufficiently confident in their productivity to down tools when they should. If you feel like you're running just to keep up, then it's hard to do a good job or motivate others. As Smiles puts it: *'The miscalculation of time involves us in perpetual hurry, confusion, and difficulties, and life becomes a mere shuffle of expedients, usually followed by disaster.'*

Granted, that sounds like a description of any given Monday for most of us, but the real culprit here is more likely to be time management than the genuine workload. If you're always working on urgent, short-term activities and you are not a surgeon in ER then you may need to examine whether you, or your organisation's work practices, are really being applied effectively.

Conduct your own mini time-and-motion study into the way you work. Consultants like to mention the Pareto principle, which assesses that 80% of the results come from just 20% of your effort. Conversely, a full 80% of your time is wasted on achieving just 20% of the work. Obviously, the goal is to find that 20% that pays off so well, and try to ditch as much of the rest as you can. The first part of that little miracle is to analyse just what it is you're doing with your day.

If you find that an hour a day goes on Solitaire and Facebook, then that's a pretty good starting point to eliminate your own time-wasting activities. If you find that a lot of your week is wasted because you are waiting for results from some other person or part of the organisation, then make absolutely sure of your facts and point it out to them because it suggests an inefficiency in the workflow. Finally, if you have studied your every hour and concluded that you just don't have enough time to do the work, then take that paperwork to HR and suggest that maybe it's time to hire some help.

HERE'S AN IDEA FOR YOU...

Before any meeting ask yourself 'what value do I bring to this meeting, or what value does it bring for me?' If there is no good answer, decline the invitation or delegate. Encourage others to do the same and put a stop to the culture of meetings for meetings' sake.

44 PUNCTUALITY

'He who holds to his appointment and does not keep you waiting for him, shows that he has regard for your time as well as for his own,' is one of Smiles' classic observations.

DEFINING IDEA...

Punctuality is the stern virtue of men of business, and the graceful courtesy of princes.

~ EDWARD BULWER-LYTTON, BRITISH STATESMAN AND NOVELIST

Smiles deplores time wasting as literally frittering away life, and accordingly praises punctuality as showing the appropriate respect for such a precious material. *'Lost wealth may be replaced by industry, lost knowledge by study, lost health by temperance or medicine, but lost time is gone for ever. A proper consideration of the value of time will also inspire habits of punctuality. "Punctuality," said Louis XIV, "is the politeness of kings." It is also the duty of gentlemen, and the necessity of men of business.'*

As well as showing the appropriate respect to the preciousness of time, Smiles also notes that punctuality is a great way of making a good impression. *'Nothing begets confidence in a man sooner than the practice of this virtue, and nothing shakes confidence sooner than the want of it.'* Punctuality is not a mere detail; it is a contract, and from the observation of this commitment, Smiles argues, we can infer a lot about the trustworthiness of our business partners. *'Punctuality is one of the modes by which we testify our personal respect for those whom we are called upon to meet in the business of life... We naturally come to the conclusion that the person who is careless about time will be careless about business, and that he is not the one to be trusted with the transaction of matters of importance.'*

In short, it's not about a few minutes here or there. What matters is that someone who fails to make their appointments is disrespectful and not worthy of trust in other matters. It's a bit harsh to the modern ear, but where that view prevails it is important to be aware of it and make serious efforts to be on the dot. When George Washington's secretary was late and blamed the problem on a malfunctioning watch the president famously replied: *"Then you must get another watch, or I another secretary."* By saying that, he was doing his employee a favour because by far the more common course is for the offended party to say nothing and quietly simmer with resentment from that point onwards.

There are cultural issues around punctuality involving nationality (try enforcing punctuality in Burkina Faso) and age (younger people tend to think time is unlimited, just as they see themselves as immortal). Those with a more relaxed approach to timeliness should be aware of the seriousness of the issue to some groups. Make your appointments precise, stick to them and, no matter how relaxed the other party appears, if you do end up being late, be sure to apologise profusely.

HERE'S AN IDEA FOR YOU...

If you have a punctuality problem, the first step is to acknowledge it. Commit to being fifteen minutes early for all your appointments to take account of traffic/trains/etc. Nelson once said he owed all his success to turning up 15 minutes early.

45 BE PREPARED TO CHANGE YOUR STRATEGY

The Duke of Wellington was a Smiles favourite, not just for his success but for his ability to react to the situation and adapt his strategy accordingly. In the Iberian Peninsula campaign, when Wellington saw that he could not destroy the French army, *'he would thus, he conceived, destroy the morale of the French.'*

DEFINING IDEA...

What do you want to achieve or avoid? The answers to this question are objectives. How will you go about achieving your desired results? The answer to this you can call strategy.

– WILLIAM E. ROTHSCHILD, BANKER

Wellington's reputation as a general was built in the Indian campaigns, usually against far superior enemy numbers. His new appointment to the war against the French in Portugal and Spain therefore came as a great fillip to the British army in that conflict. On arrival he found once again that his forces were wildly outnumbered – never more than 30,000 British troops in the face of some 350,000 French. A lesser general, or a man inflated with his own reputation, might have stuck with the tactics that had served so well in India – shock attacks relying on the discipline and aggression of a small force to panic a larger, more unwieldy one. After all that was what had made his name.

There was a major difference between the two campaigns, however. The armies Wellington had faced in India were often poorly trained and formed of opportunistic coalitions of different groups with little cohesiveness or clear chains of command. The French, on the other hand, were seasoned veterans under a single commander and sharing the same language. *'How was he to contend against such immense forces with any fair prospect of success? His clear discernment and strong common sense son taught him that he must adopt a different policy from that of the Spanish generals, who were invariably beaten and dispersed whenever they ventured to offer battle in the open plains.'*

Wellington's answer was to destroy the French morale by drawing them into an unfamiliar pattern of fighting and denying them a single victory. *'He retired into Portugal, there to carry out the settled policy on which he had by this time determined. It was, to organize a Portuguese army under British officers, and teach them to act in combination with his own troops, in the mean time avoiding the peril of a defeat by declining all engagements ... When his army was ripe for action, and the enemy demoralized, he would fall upon them with all his might.'*

By using local support, and by paying for all the food his army took (Napoleon by contrast issued orders for his troops to steal theirs), Wellington subtly changed the environment to his favour. Wellington thereby and battled (and won) on his terms, not those of his vastly superior enemy. What we need to do is take a leaf from his book.

HERE'S AN IDEA FOR YOU...

The Internet is a great giant killer. Small companies with great websites can look more convincing and attractive than established players who have been slow to move online. Go over your marketing/sales targets again and try a 'what if?' analysis of moving your marketing budget online.

46 FACING UP TO FINANCIALS

Having already lauded Wellington's tactical vision and understanding of strategy, Smiles next highlights his advanced understanding of, and interest in, financial matters: *'His magnificent business qualities were everywhere felt; and there can be no doubt that, by the care with which he gave to every detail, he laid the foundations of his great success.'*

DEFINING IDEA...

The success strategies for managing money and building wealth are called 'money strategies'. By using them as a part of your day-to-day life, financial frustration and failure will become a thing of the past.

~ CHARLES J. GIVENS,
AMERICAN PERSONAL FINANCE EXPERT

Wellington used to say that if he knew anything at all he knew how to feed an army. An odd boast, you might think, for a man who might more reasonably be expected to talk about tactics, battle and blood. Much of Wellington's success, though, came from the fact that he was not afraid to focus on the less glamorous but no less important daily grind of the business of war. As Smiles says: *'He gave his attention to the minutest details of the service; and was accustomed to concentrate his whole energies, from time to time, on such apparently ignominious matters as soldiers' shoes, camp-kettles, biscuits and horse fodder.'* Small details perhaps, but scaled up they represented a vast business and Wellington appreciated that.

He neglected nothing and attended to every important detail himself, even setting up in business as a corn merchant on a large scale to feed his troops when he discovered there was no ready supply from home: *'Commissariat bills were created, with which grain was bought in the ports of the Mediterranean and in South America. When he had thus filled his magazines the over plus was sold to the Portuguese who were greatly in want of provisions. He left nothing whatever to chance, but provided for every contingency.'*

There are a number of lessons here. The first is Wellington understood that war is a business, with internal and external commodity markets. The second is that he saw the need to ensure his own supplies without dependence on others. In the late 1980s, entrepreneur Alan Sugar came to the same conclusion. He was building a business in cheap electronics and saw his already tight margins evaporate due to a worldwide shortage of semiconductors. Hence he went ahead and bought his own semiconductor manufacturing plants in the Far East to guarantee his supplies and pricing.

Wellington understood the importance of the financial details of his campaign. Often those working in marketing, HR, or the more creative arms of business seem to take pride in not dealing with the details of finance, but then those people are also unlikely to find themselves on the board. We should take a tip from the Iron Duke and be prepared to go face to face with the financials if we want to truly claim that we understand our own business.

HERE'S AN IDEA FOR YOU...

Learn to read a balance sheet. This may sound like a strange suggestion if you're not in finance but just understanding the terminology will give you valuable ammunition when it comes to discussing your department or activities with the bean counters. Learn to talk the language of the balance sheet and you will be taken more seriously.

47 ACCURACY ABOVE ALL

'Too little attention, however, is paid to this highly important quality of accuracy,' laments Smiles. For him, it is one of the marks of greatness, whatever field it is applied to.

Smiles reels off his favourite virtues like a roll-call of the seven dwarves: *'Attention, application, accuracy, method, punctuality, and despatch, are the principal qualities required for the efficient conduct of business of any sort.'* Of these, accuracy is probably the one most under attack these days. Emails and texting have left us unsure of whether we need to bother with correct spelling and punctuation, and the drive for despatch often means that details are left tumbling in the dust behind enterprises speeding ever faster.

DEFINING IDEA...
Fast is fine, but accuracy is everything.
– XENOPHON, GREEK HISTORIAN

Even Smiles acknowledges that such attributes can seem petty but, there again, as he puts it: *'These, at first sight, may appear to be small matters; and yet they are of essential importance to human happiness, well-being, and usefulness.'* In the case of accuracy, rather like punctuality, Smiles sees the habit as being an indicator of more profound values: *'In business affairs, it is the manner in which even small matters are transacted, that often decides men for or against you. With virtue, capacity, and good conduct in other respects, the person who is habitually inaccurate cannot be trusted; his work has to be gone over again; and he thus causes an infinity of annoyance, vexation, and trouble.'*

Smiles defines accuracy as the attention to detail, and we have seen elsewhere the importance he attaches to the small details in life. He also feels that it is part of making your own luck and in that he has the backing of modern researchers who believe that one of the biggest factors in being 'lucky' is simply having the power of observation and awareness to seize on chances that present themselves. *'It is the result of every-day experience, that steady attention to matters of detail lies at the root of human progress; and that diligence, above all, is the mother of good luck.'* Accuracy, then, is one of the routes to business bliss. *'What is done in business must be well done, for it is better to accomplish perfectly a small amount of work, than to half-do ten times as much.'*

When Lynne Truss started her newspaper column on the irritation of poor punctuation in shop signs, it seemed a quirky subject. Such was the groundswell of people joining in her complaints of poor punctuation that he subsequent book, *Eats, Shoots & Leaves* became a best-seller. It turned out that even in this day and age something as minute as the misplacing of an apostrophe is still seen as a sign of sloppiness or ignorance.

'Good rules may do much,' says Smiles, *'but good models far more; for in the latter we have instruction in action – wisdom at work.'* To improve your own wisdom at work, therefore, it's important to keep good company. Spend time with role models and mentors.

HERE'S AN IDEA FOR YOU...

Journalists used to be told a fact wasn't a fact unless it was backed up by two reliable sources. That's not a bad rule to abide by in these days of doing an Internet search for information and taking the first answer that seems to fit the bill. If you're not sure about the accuracy of something, then check it. Don't wing it.

48 THE COMPANY YOU KEEP

For Smiles, your choice of associates has truly life-shaping implications: *'Hence the vast importance of exercising great care in the selection of companions, especially in youth. There is a magnetic affinity in young persons which insensibly tends to assimilate them to each other's likeness.'*

'Mr Edgeworth [an Anglo-Irish politician] was so strongly convinced that from sympathy they involuntarily imitated or caught the tone of the company they frequented, that he held it to be of the most essential importance that they should be taught to select the very best models. "No company, or good company," was his motto.'

DEFINING IDEA...

The man of genius inspires us with a boundless confidence in our own powers.

~ RALPH WALDO EMERSON

This isn't just a wordy reworking of the old 'monkey see, monkey do' idea, although the good Mr Edgeworth does seem to suggest that simply being in good company would make you behave better. More important is the idea that a peer group of equals will help with mutual support and inspiration – a breakthrough by one shows the way for a breakthrough by others.

Unfortunately that tends to be as true of bad habits as of good. *'It was a remark of the famous Dr Sydenham that everybody some time or other would be the better or the worse for having but spoken to a good or a bad man.'* Dr Sydenham made his name as an expert in hysteria and venereal disease so it stands to reason that he knew a thing or two about transmissible ill-effects from social intercourse.

'Contact with the good never fails to impart good, and we carry away with us some of the blessing, as travellers' garments retain the odour of the flowers and shrubs through which they have passed.' What a lovely simile! There are those people whose company leaves us feeling more peaceful, or energetic, or inspired to try harder. Smiles tells us to seek them out. *'It is thus that the noble character always acts; we become insensibly elevated by him, and cannot help feeling as he does and acquiring the habit of looking at things in the same light. Such is the magical action and reaction of minds upon each other.'* As examples, Smiles points out that a lot of artists came together to inspire each other: Haydn and Handel, Beethoven and Chrubini, Northcote and Reynolds.

HERE'S AN IDEA FOR YOU...

Facebook and LinkedIn may be great networking tools but they don't bring the benefit of personal contact and inspiration. However, even niche businesses can set up networking sessions. Take your lead from a handful of mobile marketers I know, who persuaded a bar to offer a happy hour for people in their business. Word got around fast and it is now a monthly must-meet session.

49 CHEER UP

Appropriately, given his name, Smiles believed in being a cheerful soul. *'One of the most valuable, and one of the most infections examples which can be set before the young, is that of cheerful working.'*

DEFINING IDEA...

Sometimes your joy is the source of your smile, but sometimes your smile can be the source of your joy.

– THICH NHAT HANH, VIETNAMESE MONK AND ACTIVIST

As it happens, Smiles is so in praise of a sunny disposition that you'd think he was selling the stuff. *'Cheerfulness gives elasticity to the spirit. Spectres fly before it; difficulties cause no despair, for they are encountered with hope, and the mind acquires that happy disposition to improve opportunities which rarely fails of success. The fervent spirit is always a healthy and happy spirit; working cheerfully itself, and stimulating others to work.'*

Smiles lists some of the merry japes his otherwise worthy and serious-minded heroes have got up to: *'Granville Sharp, amidst his indefatigable labours on behalf of the slave, solaced himself in the evenings by taking part in glees and instrumental concerts at his brother's house . . . he also indulged, though sparingly [whoah – steady, tiger!], in caricature drawing.'* I shouldn't mock Smiles' heroes and their 'glees'. Given that we tend to see the Victorians as a bunch of killjoy prudes, it's a positive pleasure to hear such a leading member of the society emphasising the importance of having a smile on your face, just as long as you don't overdo it on the caricature drawing, of course.

Once again, any attribute Smiles singles out is because he feels it has an effect on our ability to apply ourselves to work, and thereby to improve ourselves. A happy worker is a better worker. A happy manager is even more effective because of that 'infectious' factor touched on by Smiles. Cheerful leaders can easily touch off a virtuous circle because colleagues who look to them for guidance (and as a weathervane for how work is going) will tend to cheer up in turn as they see their leader's happiness.

You don't have to wander around grinning like the Joker, however. Just make the effort to show a little happiness when you don't have a direct reason to be miserable. I used to know a manager who was so perpetually downbeat about his work that he came to be known as 'Eeyore'. As it happens he was great at his job, and a great guy, but he could never bring himself to enthuse about what he did. When you are the one that others look to for inspiration, it's better to be a Tigger.

HERE'S AN IDEA FOR YOU...

Happiness is a habit too. Get in the habit of looking on the bright side and it will become your nature. Take a break from bad news media stories and instead look at your own life and those you love. Studies show that asked how the country/economy/world is going, most of us say 'badly'. Asked how we are personally, most of us say 'well'.

50 TRAIN, DON'T TELL

'The best teachers,' Smiles informs us, *'. . . have relied more upon training than upon telling, and sought to make their pupils themselves active parties to the work in which they were engaged.'*

DEFINING IDEA...

When planning for a year, plant corn. When planning for a decade, plant trees. When planning for life, train and educate people.

~ CHINESE PROVERB

Smiles makes a big deal of the superiority of action over words so it shouldn't come as too much of a surprise when he stresses the importance of training rather than teaching. Given the context of the Victorian approach to education, with its dour dogma and authoritarian preaching, it is a refreshing message and another which holds true over time. Telling somebody how to do something is only effective with those who are already motivated to learn. Showing somebody and involving them in the process as they go makes teaching *'something far higher than the mere passive reception of the scraps and details of knowledge.'*

Simply giving people the information doesn't mean they do anything about it. In the UK we were compulsorily taught French in school up to the age of sixteen and yet the vast majority of us still couldn't order a beer and a bag of peanuts if our monoglot little lives depended on it. Nor is that a reflection of the quality of education.

Too many people still think that the process of learning takes place through some kind of osmosis – if they attend the lesson they will therefore understand the subject. Smiles lauds the practice of educator Dr Arnold who *'strove to teach his pupils to rely upon themselves, and develop their powers by their own active efforts, himself merely guiding, directing, stimulating, and encouraging them.'*

Don't tell someone how to do something or give them instructions but sit down and do it together. Don't even see it as training – just get other people involved in what you're doing. I had a colleague who used to go through her 'to do' list with her assistant, discussing how to handle each point. The colleague did it because discussing the issues out loud helped her decide how to address them, but in the process she was also passing on her thinking and problem-solving abilities to her assistant. There was no formal training involved, but the end result was a far more useful assistant to whom the manager could later delegate with confidence. Unsurprisingly the assistant is now a senior manager and returning the favour by passing his learning on to his assistant and associates in the same way. Train people rather than tell people and they will grow under your tutelage, giving you associates who can genuinely help you out when the pressure is on.

HERE'S AN IDEA FOR YOU...

Don't have enough time to train someone? Quicker to do it yourself? Then you'd better like doing that because you're always going to be doing it yourself and you're always going to be in a rush. Break the cycle by training up some help.

51 CULTIVATE GOOD HABITS

'Man, it has been said, is a bundle of habits; and habit is second nature.' Smiles didn't believe in good acts in isolation. He felt that we are such creatures of habit that if we can cultivate good habits instead of bad then we will become better people.

DEFINING IDEA...

An unfortunate thing about this world is that the good habits are much easier to give up than the bad ones.

– WILLIAM SOMERSET MAUGHAM

'Metastastio entertained so strong an opinion as to the power of repetition in act and thought that he said, "All is habit in mankind, even virtue itself." Butler, in his Analogy, impresses the importance of careful self-discipline and firm resistance to temptation, as tending to make virtue habitual, so that at length it may become more easy to be good than to give way to sin.' Applied to both our personal and business lives, that's a very appealing prospect – just as we can so easily slip into bad habits so we can become better people by drilling ourselves into good habits. The catch is that we all know just how much easier it is to get into bad habits than good ones. New Year's resolutions rarely make it through January, and in some cases barely make it through the first day.

Smiles, as ever, prefers to give the examples of virtuous men rather than dwell on the temptations of idleness and vice: *'Thus, make sobriety a habit, and intemperance will be hateful; make prudence a habit, and reckless profligacy will become revolting to every principle of conduct which regulates the life of the individual.'*

Mindful of the dangerous inroad of any evil habit, he adds: *'It is a fine remark of a Russian writer, that "Habits are a necklace of pearls: untie the knot, and the whole unthreads."'* Come February and most of us are looking for the pearls of good intentions under the furniture.

Smiles warns of the insidious nature of any habit formed unconsciously. *'Wherever formed, habit acts involuntarily, and without effort; and, it is only when you oppose it, that you find how powerful it has become. What is done once and again, soon gives facility and proneness. The habit at first may seem to have no more strength than a spider's web; but, once formed, it binds as with a chain of iron.'* He means that thinking 'it's OK, I can handle it' is a recipe for disaster. When making exceptions ('oh, just this once'), we need to be more wary of opening the door for a complete change in our habits since, as Smiles says, we only realise their strength when we then try to break them. The issue is to demonstrate the willpower to get out the door and get better.

HERE'S AN IDEA FOR YOU...

Good intentions stall because things can go wrong. It's going to happen, so plan for it. If you fall off the wagon/diet plan/non-smoking/work schedule then give yourself a strict limit of time before you get right back on. Agree that within two days of breaking your new habit you will try and kick-start it again.

52 BE PREPARED TO BELIEVE THE BEST OF PEOPLE

In his conclusion on the road to greatness, Smiles steps back from the usual parade of the great and the good and allows a few of life's extras to have their moment. *'Even the common soldiers proved themselves gentlemen,'* he says of the troops.

DEFINING IDEA...

People glorify all sorts of bravery except the bravery they might show on behalf of their nearest neighbours.
– GEORGE ELIOT, NOVELIST

In particular, he tells the tale of the Birkenhead, a steamer carrying troops off the coast of South Africa. There were nearly 500 soldiers on board, and 166 women and children. The ship struck a rock and began to sink. The officers called the troops to ranks and it became immediately apparent that there were nowhere near enough boats to save everyone. The word went round that the boats should be reserved for the women and children – the origin of the tradition 'women and children first' that has remained the rule at sea ever since.

It was suggested the troops should jump for the sea and take their chances but it was pointed out that the men in the water would inevitably grab for the boats and probably swamp them. So they stood on the deck, in line, and waited to die. According to one of the few survivors: *"There was not a murmur nor a cry amongst them, until the vessel made her final plunge."*

It must have taken much more than mere military discipline for those troops to give up their lives. Smiles' point is that these men, far more than those brought up with property, titles and education, were gentlemen in the truest sense of the word. *'The wreck of the Birkenhead . . . affords another memorable illustration of the chivalrous spirit of common men acting in this nineteenth century, of which any age might be proud.'* What's interesting here is that Smiles is echoing a sentiment we hear today – 'the age of chivalry is gone' we are told. Clearly the same was said in Smiles' day, too, and he is keen to deny that with examples of the common man's humanity: *'The march of Neill on Cawnpore, of Havelock on Lucknow – officers and men alike urged on by the hope of rescuing the women and the children – are events which the whole history of chivalry cannot equal.'*

In short, people are as good now as they've ever been, says Smiles, and that's true today. Believe in the inherent meanness of those around you and you will probably find them mean. Believe in their goodness and the converse is true. How much faith we put in those we work and live with is very often the difference between how well or badly they then repay it.

HERE'S AN IDEA FOR YOU...

Let people know you don't expect much from them and 'not much' is what you'll get. So, next time you're hoping your team or colleagues are going to deliver, explain why it's important that they do so. Tell them you know that if they understand the importance of this action you are 100% confident they will deliver to standard.

INDEX